Rachel Garton is a consultant solicitor for Nexa Law, specialising in property dispute resolution.

Her work comprises of all areas of property litigation and landlord and tenant matters, including: residential long leasehold, tenants right of first refusal, lease renewal litigation, commercial and residential possession proceedings and debt recovery.

She has a niche specialism in service charge disputes and has dealt with numerous service charge disputes from commercial and residential clients over the last 14 years

A Practical Guide to Residential Service Charges

Second Edition

A Practical Guide to Residential Service Charges

Second Edition

Rachel Garton

BSC (Hons), LL.Dip, LL.PgDip

Law Brief Publishing

Published 2026 by Law Brief Publishing, an imprint of Law Brief Publishing Ltd
30 The Parks
Minehead
Somerset
TA24 8BT

www.lawbriefpublishing.com

Paperback: 978-1-918241-14-3

To Sawyer, Jacob, Ethan, Lilah,

Ethan, Ember and Willow

PREFACE

With the number of residential service charge disputes rising, this work is intended to serve as a simple guide to the key issues for practitioners. Each chapter provides insight into points that commonly arise and aims to provide guidance necessary to assist in a residential service charge dispute.

The main focus of this book is on section 20 consultations being the largest area of contention but touches on other residential issues that should be considered.

This book endeavours to summarise the current law on residential service charges as of 31 October 2025. It firstly deals with general principles and then focuses on the statutory controls that are applicable to residential service charges. It ends by dealing with service charge disputes, the possible remedies available and possible future changes in the legislation.

Rachel Garton
December 2025

CONTENTS

PART ONE

GENERAL PRINCIPLES APPLICABLE TO SERVICE CHARGES

Part 1 of this book aims to provide guidance on some general principles that practitioners, landlords and tenant should be aware of when dealing with residential service charges. The main area discussed is the importance of the wording of the service charge clause and what should be included and provided for within that wording.

Part 1 then progresses to discuss the importance of complying with the requirements under the service charge clause and other factors which may need to be considered in assessing if service charges are payable.

The principles set out in this part are based on both commercial and residential property case law and are thought to apply to both sectors. Whether each of the principles applies will depend on the facts of each individual case.

CHAPTER ONE

THE CONSTRUCTION OF THE SERVICE CHARGE CLAUSE

Introduction

The drafting of a service charge clause is paramount. Even though residential service charges are subject to statutory controls, the service charge clause still needs to be appropriately drafted. A Court will look at the wording of the lease as a starting point for dealing with most disputes. In addition, a badly drafted service charge clause can lead to numerous disputes regarding interpretation which could be avoided.

The main elements of a service charge clause

The main elements of a service charge clause should be as follows: -

1. A definition of the services to be carried out.

2. Details of the landlord's obligation to provide the services.

3. Details of the tenant's obligation to contribute to the costs of providing those services.

4. The mechanics of the service charge.

Defining the services

This is usually firstly a list of services which the landlord must provide for the communal areas of the property and secondly a list of services which the landlord can but is not obliged to provide.

The services specified will depend on what is applicable to the particular property, but it should be as detailed a list as possible and aim to cover all the services that could be provided.

The lease may also contain a sweeper clause. The purpose of a sweeper clause is to effectively cover any additional services the landlord may provide which are not specified in the list of services contained in the main service charge clause.

Practitioners should be wary of the inclusion and drafting of sweeper clauses and aim to restrict the clause to being tied to the categories of services that they have specified in the main clause. Sweeper clauses are construed quite restrictively, and there is no guarantee that the inclusion of a sweeper clause will allow the landlord to recover costs for any services that become necessary, or they decide to carry out that are outside of the those provided for.

Relevant Cases

Fluor Daniel Properties Limited v Shortlands Investments Limited [2001]

Provided that sweeper clauses shouldn't be used to try and recover service charges for a service which the landlord has simply failed to provide for in the service charge clause in error.

Boldmark Limited v Cohan and another [1986]

It was held that the landlords attempt to claim interest that was incurred as a result of borrowing to finance the provision of services was not recoverable under a sweeper clause that provided for recovery of service charges for general administration and management of the property.

89 Park (Management Limited) v Dell and Dell [2023]

The landlord tried to claim the costs of proceedings against the property owner of neighbouring land from the tenants under the service charges provisions. The tenants had the benefit of restrictive covenants over the neighbouring land and the proceedings were to stop planning permission for a modern residential development which the tenants opposed. The landlord relied on the wording of the sweeper clauses in the tenants' leases which stated the landlord was entitled to recover costs for the proper maintenance safety amenity and administration of the building. The Court of Appeal found that the service charge clauses were in relation to the building not the neighbouring land and therefore the costs of the proceedings in respect of the land fell outside of the service charge provisions.

Landlord's obligation to provide the services

It is crucial that a service charge clause sets out that the landlord is obliged to carry out the services detailed. If not, a tenant is potentially left living in a property where the common areas may fall into disrepair.

There is sometimes an obligation on a landlord to carry out some services and then a clause that sets out the services the landlord can provide if they choose. In respect of the latter the tenant will be under an obligation to pay for those services if carried out, but the landlord does not have to carry out those services.

The clause can set out that the landlord's obligation to carry out the works are conditional on the tenant paying the service charge due. However, practitioners should be aware that this may not be enforceable if other tenant have paid their service charge contributions. In addition, a Court is likely to be reluctant to allow a landlord to withhold services which are considered essential (*Yorkbrook Investments Limited -v- Batten [1986]*)

Tenant's obligation to contribute to the service charge

This clause should state that the tenant is obliged to pay for the services set out and

deal with the below.

The apportionment of the service charge

The apportionment of service charges between the tenant is usually one of the following:

- By way of fixed proportions. This method provides certainty. However, it is quite inflexible and can be unfair if the building is later developed/extended. If the fixed proportion is a percentage, tenants should also be wary as if any of the flats in the property are not let, they are likely to have to pay a higher sum towards the service charges unless provision has been specifically made for this occurrence.

- The tenant is asked to pay a fair proportion. This method of apportionment is likely to lead to disputes because what is 'fair' is open for interpretation. What a landlord and tenant consider to be a fair proportion is likely to differ.

- By reference to floor areas. Although to a degree this method seems fairer it can sometimes be difficult to calculate.

- By reference to rateable value. Again, this seems one of the fairer methods but can cause problems if the property is a new build and no rateable values have been set or in cases where there have been any improvements to the property.

As can be seen from the above, specifying how service charges are to be apportioned is a difficult task. Disputes can arise no matter which method is used, and all practitioners can do is try and choose the method which appears to be the most fair and reasonable for the particular property.

Relevant case

Aviva Investors Ground Rent GP Ltd and another v Williams and others [2021]

This case concerned a block of 69 residential flats and a commercial unit where the leases required the tenants to pay service charges that was stated to be a fixed percentage or a proportion to be reasonably determined by the landlord. Once the residential and commercial units ceased to be in common ownership the fixed percentages no longer allowed the landlord to fully recover its costs. Therefore, the landlord started to claim service charges in different proportions to the fixed percentages set out in the leases. The tenants argued that because of section 27A(6) of the Act the clause that allowed the landlord to charge anything other than the fixed percentage was invalid. A few years after the landlord started charging the different proportions, a group of tenants sought to challenge this practice and lodged an Application to Section 27A(1) of the Act. The Court held that the service charge clause in the leases that gave the landlord the ability to vary the percentage was not void. However, any variation would still be subject to reasonableness and could be reviewed by the First Tier Tribunal.

Bradley v Abacus Land 4 Limited [2024]

It was held that, where the landlord was required to act reasonably when exercising its discretion on the apportionment of service charge costs, the requirement was to act with objective reasonableness. However, if there was no requirement for the landlord to act reasonable the test to be applied one of rationality only.

How tenants are to pay the service charges

The service charge clause needs to set out how the tenant is to pay the service charges. The usual way is for the tenant to make quarterly payments on account during each service charge year.

The clause should also provide for any additional sums that may become due at the year-end due to a shortfall once the service charge accounts have been finalised or any surplus of funds at the year end.

The Mechanics of the Service Charge

For any workable service charge clause there needs to be provision for the following: -

1. The Service charge year – the tenant needs to know the period for the service charge accounts are to be prepared.

2. Provision for the statement of account to be prepared. This needs to set out who is to prepare the statement and who is to certify the statement. It is important that the landlord then follows this requirement to avoid the statement of account being invalid and providing a defence to the payment of the service charges that have arisen.

3. A timetable for preparing the service charge accounts. This can just be a requirement for the landlord to provide the accounts as soon as reasonably possible if the landlord is concerned about being tied down to a strict period. The important thing for landlords to note is that there shouldn't be excessive delay and a period of approx. 4 months after the end of the service charge year is usually deemed reasonable.

4. How any disputes regarding the service charges are to be dealt with. This will normally set out if there is to be a referral to a third party.

The Court's interpretation of a Service Charge Clause

A Court is unlikely to imply a term into a service charge clause or construe the express terms of a service charge clause in a different way to take into consideration commercial sense or to remedy the fact that a party has signed up to a bad deal.

Relevant cases

Arnold v Britton [2005]

The lease contained a service charge clause which provided for a fixed annual charge of £90 for the first year of the term and it was to increase each subsequent year by 10% on a £1 basis. This meant that in 2072, the tenants would be liable to pay a service charge for over £550,000. The tenants argued this could not have been what was intended. The court held that the service charge clause was clear, and it was not for the Court to step in and imply a term to prevent the tenant from having to pay the contractual terms due. The fact it was a really bad deal for the tenants was irrelevant in interpreting the clause.

Marks & Spencers Plc v BMP Paribas Securities Trust Company (Jersey) Limited [2015]

The lease contained a break clause which had a pre-condition that there should be no rent arrears. The tenant exercised their right under the break to terminate the lease on 24 January 2012. The rent was due on the usual quarter dates, and the tenant paid the full quarters rent on 25 December 2011 in order to comply with the pre-condition that there should be no rent arrears. The tenant then requested the overpayment of rent for the period after the lease was terminated from 25 January 2012 to 24 March

2012. It was held that the landlord did not have to refund the overpayment for when the tenant was no longer in occupation as there was no express obligation for the landlord to do so.

Summary

The drafting of the service charge clauses is crucial to ensure that the provision of services and payment for those services runs smoothly. Neither party is likely to be able to imply a term into the service charge clause at a later date because they were unsure of the meaning and/or have realised they have signed up to a bad deal. Nor is a landlord likely to be able to claim service charges for services which they have omitted from the drafting in error.

CHAPTER TWO

COMPLYING WITH THE MECHANICS OF A SERVICE CHARGE CLAUSE

Introduction

Having set out the mechanics of the service charge in the lease the parties, and in particular the landlord, need to ensure they comply with any requirements in the lease to ensure they can recover service charges from the tenant and avoid a dispute over liability.

Contractual machinery

If a lease provides contractual machinery, the landlord must comply with this machinery, or the service charges are unlikely to be payable. Contractual machinery is likely to be in relation to the provision of service charge accounts and/or service charge estimates, how service charges payments are to be held and dates payment are to be made.

A number of cases have shown that a landlord will need to rectify any error they have made by failing to comply with the requirements of a service charge clause and also that the landlord may not be able to recover service charges from tenants if the contractual machinery has not been observed.

A common issue is when a managing agent takes over the running of a property and fails to review the lease and the requirements thereunder prior to using the accounting equipment/programmes they currently own. It may seem more time intensive to a landlord or a management company in the short term to review the leases of the development and implement any requirements but in the long term it can prevent disputes about whether service charges are payable. In turn this can avoid significant losses for the landlord/management company if the service charges are not deemed recoverable.

Relevant cases

St Mary's Mansions Limited v Limegate Investment Co. Limited [2003]

The leases for a block of flats provided for a reserve fund for any anticipated expenditure. The landlord was transferring surplus payments that were being paid into the service charge account into the reserve fund. It was held that as the lease only provided for sums in the reserve fund to be anticipated expenditure only the sums held in the reserve fund for recurring expenditure had been properly allocated. The landlord had to repay or credit any surplus to the tenants at the end of each service charge year. The judge stated that compliance with contractual machinery in the leases is not optional, it is compulsory.

Jacey Property Company Limited v De Sousa [2003]

The landlord sought possession of the property and one of the grounds they were relying on to forfeit the lease was that the tenant had failed to pay the costs due in respect of work carried out to the drains. The lease provided that the tenant was to pay a proper and fair portion as determined by the landlord's surveyor of the expense of repairing, renewing and rebuilding the sewers and drains. The landlord had claimed service charges from the tenant for the works carried out, but the landlord had the portion payable determined by their solicitor not their surveyor as provided for in the lease. The tenant disputed that the sum was payable as it the potion payable had not been determined by the landlord's surveyor. The tenant was successful and it was held that it is not for the landlord to decide to use anyone other than a surveyor even if they chose an appropriately skilled person as an alternative. The tenant did not need to contribute to the works carried out on the drains and the landlord could not rely on this ground to terminate the lease.

Barrington v Sloane Properties [2007]

The landlord carried out substantial building works between 2000 and 2003. The leases of the block of flats provided that the tenants would pay 24.24% of the actual costs of the landlord but that the sums due had to be certified annually by the landlord's accountant. The landlord's accountant apportioned and certified the costs of the works for each service charge year on the basis of an estimate of the value of the works carried out. The Court held that the certificates were not binding as the accountant had not taken into consideration the actual costs that the landlord has to pay in each service charge year. The lease had been misinterpreted and the landlord was therefore not entitled to recover the sums due.

Condition Precedent

A Condition Precedent effectively sets out the events that must occur before liability for service charges can arise. This is similar to contractual machinery but can appear in lease in addition to contractual machinery and again is something that landlords need to be very careful they comply with to avoid a challenge from tenants regarding payment.

Relevant Case

Quirkco Investments Limited -v- Aspray Transport Ltd [2011]

The tenant served a break notice to terminate the lease. The landlord argued the break was ineffective as they had not paid the services charges due in respect of the insurance premium. The lease set out that the landlord should only demand service charges in respect of insurance charges once the landlord had paid the premium. The landlord had not paid the premium when he demanded payment of the charges. The court held that as the landlord had not paid the premium the charges were not due from the tenant. The tenant had validly exercised the break in the lease and the lease would terminate on the date specified in the notice.

Summary

If there are provisions in the lease, they must be strictly complied with. Failure to do is likely to result in either a further administrative burden in trying to rectify the error or a financial loss.

CHAPTER THREE

GENERAL FACTORS TO CONSIDER IN DETERMINING WHETHER THE SERVICE CHARGES CLAIMED ARE PAYABLE UNDER THE LEASE

Introduction

It is common sense that the landlord can only claim costs by way of service charges for the services specified in the lease. A landlord should therefore ensure that he only carries out works for which he can recover payment and a tenant should check that the landlord isn't charging them for works outside of those payable under the service charge clause. As set out in Chapter 1, the landlord may try and rely on sweeper clauses but there is no guarantee this will be successful.

In addition to whether the works are covered under the service charge clause, landlords also need to ensure that they take into consideration / be aware of the following.

Repairs or Improvements

Sometimes improvements can be covered in the service charge clause. Whether they are included usually comes down to the bargaining power of the parties. Usually, they will be excluded, and landlords need to be careful that service charges claimed are for repairs not improvements, if improvements are not covered under the service charge clause. There are frequent disputes about what is a repair and what is an improvement and this area of law is far from clear. A few cases are set out below to aid in assessing whether works are an improvement or a repair, but it is stressed that any finding by a Court or Tribunal will be highly dependent on the facts of the particular case.

Relevant Cases

Fluor Daniel Properties Limited v Shortlands Investments Limited [2001]

The landlord replaced the air conditioning units. The Court held this was an improvement not a repair. However, it is important to note that the air conditioning unit was still working when it was replaced. The Court may have held the replacement of the air conditioning unit to be a repair if the air conditioning unit had been in a state of disrepair and needed replacing.

Craighead v Home for Islington Ltd [2010]

It was held that replacement single glazed windows with double glazed windows were repairs not improvements. On first thought, you would consider this an improvement as it is effectively an upgrade. However, now all new homes have double glazed windows as standard and it is reasonable if a landlord is going to repair single glazed windows to upgrade them to what is now the norm.

Tedworth North Management Limited v Miller [2016]

The Court held that wooden frames being replaced with metal frames was an improvement. They said that the old frames only needed small scale repair not replacing. The works went above what was needed in the circumstances.

Service Charge Cap

Service charges can be capped imposing a restriction on the amount that can be charged by a landlord to the tenant in any service charge year. If there is a service charge cap in place, landlords should not try and get round this restriction.

Relevant Case

Princes House Ltd & Another v Distinctive Clubs Ltd [2007].

The service charge clause included a cap on the recovery in the first 5 years of the lease. The landlord informed the tenant that they would be carrying out works to the roof within the first 5 years. The landlord then stated the works would take longer than envisaged and would not be within the first 5 years. The landlord then looked to claim the costs in full as they had avoided the service charge cap. The tenant disputed the sums were due as they were a result of the landlord purposely delaying. The landlord's defence was that their obligation to do the works was qualified by a liability clause stating that the landlord would not be liable to the tenant in respect of their failure to carry out maintenance and repair duties until the tenant had notified the landlord of such a failure. The landlord argued that the tenant had not sent any notification to them. It was held that the landlord was fully aware of the need to do the works as they had informed the tenant of their intention to carry out the works. The landlord could not now rely on the liability clause. The works should have been carried out within the 5-year window and were subject to the service charge cap. The landlord could not simply delay works to avoid the cap.

Estoppel by convention

The general rule of interpretation of a service charge clause is set out in the chapters above i.e., if the landlord does not comply with the service charge provisions strictly, the service charges are unlikely to be due. However, there is the possibility of an argument in some rare cases that if a tenant has conceded the landlord's failure to comply with the service charges provisions for a duration of time the tenant is estopped from objecting to this error.

Relevant Case

Admiralty Park Management Limited v Ojo [2016]

There was an error in the landlord's calculations of service charge due and they sent non-compliant service charge demands to the tenants for a period of 5 years from 2009 to 2014. The lease provided that the service charge payable should be calculated by dividing the total charge for each block of flats by the number of flats within that block. Instead, the landlord had been dividing the total charge for the whole estate by the number of flats in the estate. The number of flats in each block varied so the landlord had been using the wrong apportionment. Although the tenant had been paying the sums demanded since 2009, he stopped paying in 2014 and argued the sums claimed were not payable due to the landlord's error. It was held that the sums claimed were still payable. The tenant was estopped by convention from objecting as they had accepted the error without protest for several years. This case was a fascinating development as it showed it is possible for a party's conduct to effectively vary the requirements under the lease. Despite this case, an argument on estoppel by convention should be raised with caution. It will be highly dependent on the facts and in particular how long the error has been ongoing and when the tenant became aware of the error.

Summary

When looking to carry out works under the lease, the landlord needs to double check that the costs that they are looking to recover are covered by the provisions in the lease and are also that they are likely to be able to recover the sums claimed in light of the principles above. The general principles discussed need to be looked at alongside the facts of the case and the statutory controls discussed later in this book.

PART TWO

STATUTORY REGULATIONS FOR RESIDENTIAL SERVICE CHARGES

Part 1 has dealt with the general law and some general principles on service charge clauses. These issues apply to commercial and residential service charges equally and are a crucial starting point. However, residential service charges are also subject to legislation and statutory controls which require landlords to consult with tenants for certain works and services as well as set out requirements and limitations for what landlords can recover as service charges. Part 2 aims to deal with some of the key legislative requirements as well as key considerations when dealing with residential service charges. The matters dealt with are not an exhaustive list of what a practitioner should consider but aim to aid and assist in considering service charges disputes.

The issues discussed are on the assumption that the Landlord and Tenant Act 1985 ('the Act') applies to both the residential tenancy and the service charges claimed. Public Sector tenancies (unless it is a long tenancy as defined by section 26 of the Act) and Rent Control tenancies do not have the protection of the Act. All other residential tenancies will have the protection of the Act in respect of service charges as long as the amount claimed falls within the definition of service charges set out at section 18 of the Act.

Section 18 of the Act defines service charge as an amount which is payable by the tenant of a dwelling as part of or in addition to rent, is payable for a service, repairs, maintenance, improvement, insurance or management costs and is a charge that can vary. If the service charge payable is fixed by the lease, they are not subject to the Act.

CHAPTER FOUR

SECTION 20 CONSULTATIONS: PURPOSE AND APPLICATION

Introduction

Section 20 of the Act (as amended by Section 151 of the Commonhold Leasehold Act 2002 ('CLARA 2002') provides that tenants paying variable service charges must be consulted before a landlord carries out qualifying works or enters into a long-term agreement for the provision of services.

Detailed regulations have been produced under Section 20 which set out the precise procedures which a landlord must follow. These are the Service Charges (Consultation Requirements) Regulations 2003 ('the Regulations').

It is clear to see the purpose and reasoning behind introducing section 20 consultations. It makes sense that landlords should consult tenants as they are the ones effected by the works and ultimately liable for the cost of the works and it aims to foster a good working relationship between the parties. However, section 20 consultations result in a significant amount of litigation and the requirements under the Act and Regulations are a huge area of contention. Issues arise as many landlords fail to consult when they should or make mistakes in the process giving tenants the opportunity to dispute that payment is due.

When is a Section 20 Consultation Required?

A Section 20 Consultation is required in 2 scenarios. Firstly, qualifying works over £250 to any one tenant and secondly under qualifying long-term agreements. Consultation applies to all landlords, resident management companies and right to manage companies.

Qualifying Works over £250.00 for any one tenant

Qualifying works are works on the building or any other premises that is works of repair, maintenance and improvement.

To be qualifying works, the works must be of a value that is over £250 for any one tenant. In a property with unequal service charge contributions the landlord must consult all tenants if one of them would have to pay more that £250.

Cost thresholds in the Regulations are subject to change from time to time by the Secretary of State However, they do not seem to vary very often, and the current threshold had been in place since the Regulations came into force.

Relevant Cases

Francis & Others v Phillips & Others 2014

This case dealt with the definition of qualifying works and how it applies to works done by the landlord and whether the definition incorporated all of the works carried out over a year period. The case caused lots of confusion and has been very controversial.

There were 150 holiday chalets let on long leases in Cornwall. The landlord charged the tenants £3,117.47 per chalet for the works they had carried out throughout the service charge year. The landlord did not carry out a section 20 consultation as the amount charged did not relate to a single set out works but was the accumulated total for a number of works.

Lower Court decision: The works undertaken were not a single set of qualifying works so therefore a consultation was not necessary. Payment of the service charge was due to the landlord.

High Court decision: The threshold applied to the accumulated costs of all the works and services within the relevant service charge period not just a single set of qualifying works. As the works carried out over the service charge period added up to more than £250 per tenant, a consultation was necessary. Service charge payments were not due to the landlord as they had not carried out the required consultation process.

Court of Appeal decision: The Court of Appeal overturned the decision of the High Court and reinstated the belief that the service charge threshold applied to a single set of qualifying works not to the aggravated costs of all works and services within the relevant service charge period.

This case also discussed the factors a Court may look at to determine whether the works carried out by the landlord are a single set of qualifying works. The factors that may be taken into consideration are as follows: -

a) Where items of work are to be carried out?

b) Whether the works are subject to the same contract?

c) Whether the works are to be done at more or less the same time or at different times?

d) Whether the type of works to be carried out are different in character from the other works that have been carried out in the same service charge period or if there is any connection between the different sets of work.

e) How the works are planned and the reasons for how they are to implemented.

It is important to note that this is not an exhaustive list, and a Court will consider the facts of each individual case to decide if the works are a single set of works and subject to consultation or separate works that are not subject to consultation.

Qualifying Long Term Agreements

Qualifying Long Term Agreements ('QLATAS') are agreements that are:-

a) more than twelve months in length and.

b) cost any one tenant over £100 in a year. As with qualifying works it doesn't matter if the works costs under £100 for the majority of the tenants. As long as the cost is over £100 for one tenant it will qualify as a QLATA.

Examples of QLATAS would be maintenance agreements for utilities , agreements for lifts and waste management, insurance agreements and management agency agreements.

It doesn't matter if the service provider is the only realistically possible supplier. The consultation process still needs to be followed unless dispensation is obtained. Dispensation is discussed below.

There are some exclusions to agreements over a year that are not QLATAs. These are: -

a) Employment contracts.

b) Management agreements between a local housing authority and a tenant management organisation under the Housing Act 1985 or a body established under the Local Government Act 2000.

c) Contracts between companies in the same group.

d) Contracts for not more than five years entered into when the tenants were in the property.

e) Contracts pre-31 October 2003. These are discussed below.

Relevant Cases

Paddington Basin Developments Ltd & Others v West End Quay Estate Management Limited [2010]

Paddington Basement Developments Limited ('Paddington') was an estate management company party to over £400 leases of residential flats. Paddington entered into an agreement by way of an estate management deed for a minimum period of 25 years. Paddington didn't carry out any section 20 consultation and charged the costs of the deed to the tenant. The tenant argued that the service charges were not payable as it was a QLTA and a section 20 consultation had not been carried out. It was held that the deed was a QLTA. The estate management deed was an agreement because it contained contractual rights and obligations that bound the parties and was for a term of over 12 months. The landlord should have consulted the tenants under section 20 of the Act. Due to the landlord's failure to do so costs arising under the agreement were capped at the threshold of £100 per tenant.

Poynders Court Ltd v GLS Property Management Limited [2012]

Poynders Court Limited entered into a management agreement which contained no termination date or term. The agreement was subject to an annual fee which was subject to review after two years and then annually. Each party was able to terminate the agreement on 3 months' written notice. It was held that the management agreement was a QLTA as the parties intended the service to be provided for a period beyond the 12-month threshold.

Corvan (Properties) Ltd v Abdel -Mahmoud [2018]

Corvan entered into a management agreement which stated that it "will be for a period of one year from the date of signature thereof and will continue thereafter until terminated upon three months' notice from either party". It was held that the management agreement was a QLTA. The use of "and will continue" meant that the agreement would continue beyond the initial 12 months. This case raises some concerns as many building contracts have provisions where the contractors are to come back to check the work or make good defects after the contract has completed. Landlords need to be careful with the wording to ensure this type of agreement is not being treated as being over 12 months and therefore a QLTA.

Bracken Hill Court at Ackworth Management Company Limited v Dobson [2018]

The management company entered into an oral contract with managing agents to provide management services at the property. The contract was to last no longer than 364 days but was renewed for a number of years annually over the telephone. It was held that this was not a QLTA. Even though the contract was renewed on a proper construction of the wording the contract was under a 12-month period. There was no obligation for the management company to renew, and it would last less than a year if it was not renewed.

Ghosh v Hanover Gate Mansions Ltd & Anor [2019]

A draft contract was agreed on 12 June 2017 between the landlord and the managing agent but was not signed. The contract could not be terminated before 12 June 2018 if it had been signed. The provision of services pursuant to the draft contract commenced on 12 June 2017 and the first payment was made approximately 2 weeks later. It was found that the terms of engagement were per the unsigned contract. The question was then when the contract took effect. It was held that the draft contract took effect when performance of the services commenced on 12 June 2017. As the contract could not be terminated before 12 June 2018 the contract was over a year and it was a QLTA. Recovery of the service charges was limited to the £100 threshold.

Summary

When assessing works to be carried out or agreements to be entered into consideration needs to be given as to whether they will amount to qualifying works or a QLTA. This is not always straightforward and if there is doubt the landlord may want to urge on the side of caution and commence the consultation procedure set out in the chapter below.

CHAPTER FIVE

SECTION 20 CONSULTATIONS: THE PROCEDURE

Introduction

The Regulations separate the consultation procedures into 4 Schedules. The fourth Schedule has 2 parts so there are technically 5 scenarios covered by the Regulations. The consultation procedure required depends on which Schedule is applicable. However, the consultation procedure in all the schedules can be summarised as a 2 or 3 stage process for ease of reference. At each stage is that all notices required must be served on all the individual tenants and any recognised tenant association.

Summary of the Procedure

Stage 1 – Service of a Notice of Intention

Once a landlord or management company is aware that works need to be carried out, the first stage is to serve a Notice of Intention.

The Notice of Intention must:

- Set out the landlord's intention to do works/enter into an agreement

- Give a general description of the works/services/goods or specify a place and hours of which a description of the works proposed may be inspected. The place and hours must be reasonable. If the landlord sets out a place to inspect details of the works and a copy of the estimates if not provided. The landlord must also provide copying facilities and incur the costs of providing the same.

- State why the works/services/goods proposed need doing and reasons for wanting to enter into the agreement.

- Invite comments and observations from the tenants within thirty days.

- Where applicable, inform the tenant of their right to nominate contractor from whom the landlord should obtain an estimate.

Paragraph 1 (2), Part 2, Schedule 4 of the Regulations sets out the requirements and should be referred to in preparing and/or assessing a Notice of Intention.

Stage 2 – Notice of Estimates

The second stage of the process is to serve a Notice of Estimates. Prior to doing so the landlord/management company needs to have firstly, had regard to any observations that have been received from the tenants and secondly sought estimates from their proposed contractors and those nominated by the tenants.

Once the estimates have been received from the relevant contractors, the landlord can then proceed to serve this second notice.

The notice must contain a statement known as a paragraph (b) statement. The paragraph (b) statement must include the following:

- Details of the cost estimates, how to inspect them and invite any comments/observations in writing within thirty days. If the landlord sets out a place to inspect details of the works and a copy of the estimates if not provided. The landlord must also provide copying facilities and incur the costs of providing the same.

- At least two estimates. At least one of the two estimates set out in the notice of estimates must be from a contractor who is wholly unconnected with the landlord. The definition of wholly unconnected at paragraph 12(6) of Schedule 1 sets out that those considered connected with the landlord include spouses, cohabitees, parents, children, siblings and in-laws. It also covers any company that a connected person controls and where the proposed contractor is a partnership of whom the landlord or a close relative of the landlord is a partner. The notice must also set out any connection that any of the proposed contractors have with the landlord.

- A summary of the observations received from the tenants in response to the Notice of Intention and how the landlord has had regard to those observations.

Following service of the Notice of Estimates, the tenants again have a period of 30 days beginning with the date of the Notice of Estimate to make observations on the those estimates. The landlord must have regard to any observations made during that period.

<u>Relevant cases</u>

Ashleigh Court Right to Manage Company Ltd -v- Ms De-Nuccio and Others [2015]

In this case, Ashleigh was a management company of a block of 30 flats let on a 999-year lease in 1967. In 2012 Ashleigh carried out qualifying works to the property and provided both a note of intention and notice of estimates to the tenants. Within the notice of estimates the landlord specified that the tenants had to give Ashleigh 48 hours prior notice of their intention to inspect the costs estimates. In addition, the tenant was only able to inspect the estimates on weekdays between 9 a.m. and 12 p.m. Further, there were no contact details provided to arrange inspection nor was the registered address for Ashleigh provided. A notice of estimates is required to specify a place and time for inspection and the place and hours specified have to be reasonable. It was held that the limitations imposed upon the tenants right to inspect was not reasonable. As a result of the Landlord failure to comply Ashleigh was only able to recover the statutory threshold of £250.00 per tenant for the works carried out.

The case shows that it is crucially important for landlords/managing agents to strictly comply with the consultation requirements. If they fail to do so the landlord is likely to suffer from the shortfall which could prove very costly.

Stage 3 – Notice of Reasons for Awarding the Contract

The service of this third notice is not always applicable. It only applies if the landlord has chosen a contractor which was not nominated by the tenants and also did not provide the cheapest estimate. In this scenario it is required that the landlord serve a further notice showing that they have had regard to the tenants' responses to the Notice of estimates and also justification of why they chose that particular contractor. To show they have had regard to any comments received from the tenants they will need to summarise all the tenants' observations in respect of the estimates and set out their response to these observations.

If service of this this notice is applicable, it needs to be served within 21 days of awarding the contract.

What is the case if there is a superior landlord?

If a superior landlord is carrying out works to which the Act and Regulations apply, they have to consult with not just the intermediate landlord but all the sub-tenants.

Relevant case

The Leaseholders of Foundling Court & O' Donnell Court v The Mayor and Burgesses of the London Borough of Camden & Others [2016]

The Foundling Court and O' Donnell Court were residential blocks of flats forming part of the Brunswick Centre. Between 2000 and 2007 Allied London (Brunswick) Limited owned the freehold and London Borough of Camden were the tenant under a long lease. Part of the demise that was leased to the London Borough of Camden was the Foundling Court and O' Donnell Court. Camden were obliged under their lease with Allied London to contribute to service charges that were incurred as a result of Allied London carrying out the works due under the lease. Camden had let some of the flats on long leases. The sub tenants were to pay Camden service charges. On the 11 June 2004, Allied London served notice of intention on Camden only. They did not serve any of the undertenants. Camden forwarded the notice of intention to the relevant undertenants and invited their observations. On 24 September 2004, Allied London served a notice of estimates to Camden. Again, Camden forwarded the notice to the undertenants requesting observations within 21 days. After following the consultation process, Allied London then did the works. The works completed in 2006 but were not sufficient and further works were required to rectify the errors. Camden had paid the service charges due to Allied London but the undertenants had only made some interim payments to Camden. Due to the standard of the works, the Tenants applied to the Tribunal to determine the extent they were liable for the costs uncured. In order to assess if the undertenants were liable to pay the outstanding costs, the Upper Tribunal had to consider whether the duty to consult fell on the superior or intermediate landlord.

The Upper Tribunal held that as it was Allied London doing the works not Camden. It was therefore Allied London's responsibility to consult with the sub-tenants. Paragraph 1(1) of the schedules in the Regulations sets out that the Landlord is under a duty to consult with "each Tenant.

Where a property is sub-let “each Tenant” would include the sub-tenants. Allied London had failed to consult with the sub-tenant and could not recoup the service charges above the threshold.

The case is not only important as it clarifies the position when a head lease is in play but also poses a number of problem to superior Landlords if they do not know the identity of the sub-tenants. The case did recognise this issue and said there were 3 possible solutions:

1. The superior landlord can serve notices simply addressed to ‘the leaseholder’ or ‘the tenant’. There is no requirement for the recipient of the notices to be named. It may result in the landlord having to serve more notices than necessary, but it is worthwhile if it avoids them being unable to recover costs.

2. The superior landlord can ask the intermediate landlord for details of the sub-tenants. It is in their interests to provide this information. However, the superior landlord is relying on the intermediate to provide the correct information. If there are long leases the superior landlord could also carry out investigations with the Land Registry to see what leases are registered and see if this agrees with any information provided.

3. The superior landlord could seek dispensation (discussed below).

The simplest and cheapest approach seems to be the first option, but a superior landlord may decide to do both 1 and 2. This would aid when responses are received to assess which sub tenants are entitled to make observations in response to the notices.

The Schedules

As set out above there are 4 schedules dealing with specific scenarios. The definition and application of qualifying works and QLTAs remains the same in each schedule. The schedule that is applicable will depend on whether the landlord is carrying out works or entering into an agreement and whether the works or agreement are subject to the Public Contracts Regulations will determine which schedule is applicable to the landlord.

Overview of the Schedules

The Schedules are as follows:

Schedule 1 – QLTAS not governed by the Public Contracts Regulations

Schedule 2- QLTAS governed by the Public Contracts Regulations

Schedule 3 – qualifying works to be carried out either under a QLTA, under an agreement made by the landlord before 31 October 2003 where any of the work is carried out after 31 December 2003 or under a contract within the Public Works or Public Supply Regulations which was advertised before 31 October 2003 and where any work was carried out after 31 October 2003.

Schedule 4- Part 1 – qualifying works to be publicly advertised under the Public Contracts Regulations.

Schedule 4- Part 2 – All other qualifying works.

Schedule 1 and Schedule 4 part 2 tend to be the ones that most commonly apply. Each Schedule is dealt with more fully below.

Schedule 1

Schedule 1 deals with your normal QLTA. It applies to all QLTAs not governed by the Public Contracts Regulations. The procedure follows the procedure set out in the Summary of Procedures above including the requirement for the notice of intention to include inviting written nominations within 30 days from whom estimate should be sought.

Relevant Cases

Hounslow London Borough Council -v- Waaler [2017]

It was held that in deciding the nature and extent of any intended work or service the landlord must give more weight to the tenant's observations in response to the notices when they are incurring costs under a discretionary obligation in the lease. This finding incorporates the concept that a contractual discretion must be exercised rationally and in good faith.

Schedule 2

In this situation, a landlord should follow the same procedure and rules as set out in Schedule 1 with the exception of the following: -

- Tenders will be invited by the publication of public advertisements.
- The notice of intention does not need to seek nomination from the tenant and should instead state that they are not being sought as tenders are being invited by the publication.
- The landlord only has to prepare one estimate rather than alternative proposals.

Schedule 3

Under this schedule works are to be carried out under an existing agreement or an agreement made or advertised before 31 October 2003. This schedule is therefore not as extensive, and it is becoming increasing rare to come across this scenario. A notice of intention must still be served providing details of the works and why they are being carried out. It must also invite written observations. However, the notice just needs to set out the estimated total costs rather than invite nominations. As with all the schedules the landlord must still have regard to any observations received.

Schedule 4 – Part 1

This is similar to schedule 2 as it also involves the Public Contracts Regulations. For this reason, the notice of intention does not need to state that nominations are sought. Instead, it should state that public notice is being given so nominations are not required. The other provisions for the notice of intention remain and the landlord must as always have regard for any observations received. A notice of estimates then needs to be served with details of the proposed contract for works together with an estimate of costs. The landlord will need to have regard to any observations and respond to them.

Schedule 4 – Part 2

This part of schedule 4 deals with all qualifying works not covered by any of the other schedule. The procedure follows the procedure set out in the summary of procedures above including the requirement for the notice of intention to include inviting written nominations within 30 days from whom estimate should be sought.

Concerns have been raised and disputes have arisen regarding whether the landlord has complied with this schedule if the works they are carrying out change after the service of the notice of intention. This could happen for a number of reasons. For example, one of the proposed contractors may suggest that works are carried out differently to what was first proposed or due to delay more extensive works are required. In each case it will depend on the facts of the case and how far the works divert from that proposed. The case of *Reedbase Ltd v Fattal and others [2018]* dealt with this issue and discussed some factors that may be taken into consideration regarding the change in works. If in doubt, a landlord may wish to restart the consultation procedure to avoid a dispute.

This schedule does not apply where Schedule 1 applies. If the qualifying works to be carried out are under a QLTA, schedule 1 should be followed and the threshold of £100.00 applies.

The duration of the consultation procedure and timing

The whole consultation process can take several months to complete and at least 2 or 3 months due to the time needed after service of the notice of intention and notice of estimate to await observations and also to obtain estimates and have regard to the observations. A notice of reasons for awarding the contract may also be applicable in certain circumstances.

Timing of Notices

When serving each notice landlords need to ensure they give the tenants 30 clear days to respond and make any observations. The Act and the Regulations do not contain any provisions regarding service of notices, nor do they incorporate any particular statutory provisions on the deemed date of service of notices. Prior to serving any notices the landlord needs to review the lease to check if there are any service charge provisions to comply with. or if the lease is silent landlords should consider section 7 of the Interpretation Act 1978.

The absence of express provisions leaves the deemed service of notices very unclear. To avoid arguments regarding service landlords are advised to provide 2 or 3 days more than the 30 days provided to allow time for service. If it is deemed that not enough time had been provided for observations, it could invalidate that particular notice and the whole of the consultation procedure.

Relevant Case

Trafford Housing Trust Ltd -v- Rubinstein and others [2013]

This case included an Issue over when a section 20 consultation notice is deemed delivered.

The Judge wanted to apply Section 7 of the Interpretation Act 1978 but couldn't do so as the landlord had agreed a commercial delivery service which did not publish its expected delivery periods. In the absence of any express provision the Court fell back on the general principle that a letter is deemed served the second working day after posting.

Is there a deadline for landlords to implement the works/services specified in the notices?

There is no deadline in the Act or Regulations for the landlord to have carried out the works/services or appoint a contractor. However, landlords should be wary of too much delay as it could result in one of the following: -

- An invalid estimate. Usually, contractors will state their estimate is valid for a certain period of time. If that time has passed the landlord may need to obtain a further estimate before doing the works. There is then the risk that the cost of the works or the range of works will vary from the original estimate. If that is the case the landlord will need to consider if they have to restart the consultation procedure.

- There is a possible claim against the landlord if they have unreasonably delayed both as this may be in breach of the lease but also as it may have increased the works required if the property has deteriorated in the interim period.

Funding

Landlords should always consider funding the works before they serve the notice of intention. This is relevant to whether the landlord will be able to carry out the works without excessive delay. When the funds become available to the landlord will depend on the wording of the service charge clause. The lease could provide for payments in advance, in instalments, a reserve or sinking fund for these purposes or it could set out that provisions regarding the landlord borrowing money for the works in the first instance. Landlords should not simply serve the notices and then consider whether they can fund, and it is doubtful that a lack of funds will be a valid excuse for the landlord failing to carry out the works in a reasonable time.

Relevant case

Bluestorm Ltd v Portvale Holdings Ltd [2004]

This case indicated that a Court may allow a delay in the landlord carrying out works if there is a lack of funds and the landlord is completely reliant on the tenant's contribution to perform their services. This is more likely to be the case if it is a tenant management company.

Summary

The consultation procedure required depends on which Schedule is applicable and care should be taken to ensure that the correct Schedule is used and complied with when drafting the relevant consultation notices. Landlords should also try and be in a position to carry out the proposed works in a timely manner when they start the consultation process.

CHAPTER SIX

SECTION 20 CONSULTATIONS: DISPENSATION AND NON-COMPLIANCE

Introduction

Sometimes landlords fail to comply with the consultation procedures either through error or because it has just not been possible. In such circumstances there are consequences for the non-compliance unless the landlord applies for dispensation from the First Tier Tribunal under section 20ZA (1) of the Act.

Dispensation

Dispensation can be sought on one or more elements of the consultation process and applications for dispensation can be made in advance of the works or made retrospectively

Common circumstances where dispensation may be required

The consultation process is a long process likely to take place over several months. The implementation of the consultation process correctly either in whole or in part is therefore not always practical. Some examples of this are:

- Urgent works – If urgent works are required on the property, it is unlikely a landlord can wait a 2 or 3-month period minimum to start these works. If the landlord fails to consult for this reason, they should ensure the only works they do carry out without consultation are the urgent works and any non-urgent/ancillary works are left until the consultation process has been followed.

- A landlord is only able to obtain 1 estimate for the works – Despite reasonable attempts a landlord may only be able to get 1 contractor to provide an estimate for the required works. As a result, they would not be able to comply with the requirement to provide 2 estimates on the notice of estimates.

- Bulk contracts – This can arise when landlords want to enter into bulk contracts with utility companies and it is not practical for the landlord to consult with all of their tenants. This is only likely to be a possibility with landlords with a huge number of properties such as the Council.

<u>What does the Court consider when reviewing applications of dispensation?</u>

When the Tribunal deals with an application for dispensation, they will consider what prejudice has been caused to the tenants as a result of the landlord failure to consult against the landlord's circumstances. For example, in the case of bulk contracts it may be a huge, unmanageable expensive task for the landlords to consult and there may be no prejudice to the tenants by the landlord's failure to consult as the tenants are likely to be getting a better deal as a result of the bulk contract.

<u>Relevant Cases</u>

Daejan v Benson [2013]

The landlord had not ignored the consultation procedure but had failed to carry out the last stage correctly. Dispensation was granted but the Tribunal reduced the liability of the tenant by what they deemed to be the prejudice to the tenant for the landlord's failure to consult correctly. If the landlord had consulted correctly, a cheaper contractor may have been awarded the contract. On the basis of the evidence and looking at costs of alternative contractors, dispensation was granted but they reduced the sums due from the tenants by £50,000 and £220,000 was payable rather than £270,000.

OM Property Management Ltd v Burr [2014]

There was an error in the notice of estimates and in the way the landlord dealt with the tenants' observations. Dispensation was granted and the tenants were liable to pay the full sums claimed despite the errors. The finding was based on the fact that the errors did not cause any prejudice to the tenants.

Aster Communities v Chapman and others [2021]

The landlord sent a notice of intention to all the tenants, but the notice was deficient as it failed to include a part of the works required. The landlord applied for dispensation. The guidance in *Daejan* was applied and dispensation was granted subject to the landlord having to pay the reasonable costs of an expert to consider and advise the tenants on the works omitted from the notice of intention. The landlord also had to pay the tenant's reasonable cost of the application for dispensation.

How do the above cases differ from the previous approach?

The above cases are a huge relief to landlords. Before *Daejan v Benson [2013]* there was an automatic inference that the landlord's failure to comply had caused prejudice to the tenant. Now it is of the tenant to show that there has been some prejudice and the likely amount of that prejudice. Landlords are therefore less likely to be penalised for small administrative mistakes which would not affect the costs to the tenant.

Non-Compliance

If the landlord does not complete the consultation process correctly and does not seek or obtain dispensation, they are left in a situation where they are barred from recovering any service charges from the tenants towards the sums incurred for the works/services above the amount of the relevant financial threshold. The financial thresholds are:

- No more than £100.00 per year for QLTAs.
- No more than £250.00 towards the cost of qualifying works.

In the case of *Paddington Basin Developments Ltd & Others v West End Quay Estates Management Co Ltd service* charges due from the tenant were capped in this way.

In this scenario, the Landlord will have to cover the remainder of the loss himself. This could render a landlord or management company insolvent and unable to fulfil their obligations to the Tenant. This is even more likely to be the case where there is Right to Manage Company or Resident Management Company.

Summary

It is crucial that landlords take care to ensure compliance with the consultation procedure. If for any reason the landlord is unable to comply, they should apply for dispensation as soon as they are aware of the fact that they are unable to comply or have not complied. Failure to do so could prove disastrous for the landlord or management company.

CHAPTER SEVEN

REASONABLENESS

Introduction

The Act provides that costs claimed by way of service charges must be reasonable. This requirement of reasonableness also applies to advance payments, administration charges and management fees. This chapter aims to deal with how a tribunal or court is likely to assess what is reasonable to aid in assessing if there is a valid challenge to the service charges demanded on this basis.

The costs claimed by way of service charges must be reasonable

Section 19 of the Act states that the costs must be reasonable. The test for reasonableness is whether the costs have been reasonable incurred and if the works/services carried out are to a reasonable standard.

Costs must be reasonably incurred

The first part of the test for reasonableness is whether the costs incurred by the landlord have been reasonably incurred. The assessment of whether costs have been reasonably incurred is not clear cut. It is not just a matter of finding a contractor that can provide a cheaper quote for the work. A tenant will need to show that the landlord has not acted reasonably in proceeding with the contractor because the level of costs incurred is in excess of the market norm and also that there was no other justifiable reason for the landlord to have gone with this particular contractor. The length of the lease may also be relevant as a Court may be reluctant to impose high costs on a tenant with only a short-term interest in the property. The terms of the lease should be reviewed in addition to that set out below to check the landlord's conduct is in accordance with that specified. If not, it is likely to assist in arguing the costs have not been reasonable incurred.

Relevant Cases

Scottish Mutual Assurance Pc V Jardine Public Relations [1999]

The tenant had a 3-year lease with only a few months left to run when the landlord proposed to replace the roof. It was held that due to the length remaining on the lease the tenant was only liable to pay for patch work repairs. This was in respect of a commercial lease, but the principle is still relevant to the reasonableness of service charges raised in residential leases.

Fluor Daniel Properties Limited v Shortlands Investments Limited [2001]

It was found that if a landlord is to act reasonably, they will have had regard to the length of the lease.

Garside and Another v RFYC Ltd and another [2011]

This case considered the factors that could be taken into account when judging reasonableness and held that the financial impact on the tenant was a material consideration.

Oliver v Sheffield City Council [2015]

Sheffield City Council carried out extensive works to the property which included structural strengthening and the renewal of the exterior cladding. The service charge clause stated that the tenants were liable to pay the reasonable costs of the repair and improvement of the structure and exterior of the property. The tenant argued that the scope of the improvement was unreasonable, and the landlord should have carried out a more modest programme of works. The Tribunal held that the local authority had acted reasonably. The works were expensive and did include an element of improvement, but they reasonably incurred to preserve the structure and prevent deterioration of the building.

Cos Services Ltd v Nicholson and Willans [2017]

The tenant disputed that the insurance premiums charges were reasonable. The tenants provided comparable polices that were substantially lower in support of their assertion and the landlord was unable to provide any justification as to why they proceeded with an insurance premium that was higher than the market norm. It was held that the costs had not been reasonably incurred.

London Borough Council of Hounslow v Waaler [2017]

The London Borough of Hounslow carried out works in 2014. These were the replacement of a flat roof with a pitched roof and the replacement of wooden framed windows with metal frames. To do these works the Council also had to replace the external cladding and asbestos around the windows. The Tribunal had to decide if these costs had been reasonably incurred. It was held the works were an improvement rather than a repair but that there was no difference in the legal test for determining if the costs of repairs and improvements were reasonably incurred but that there was likely to be more factors for a landlord to consider when carrying out improvements. The landlord needs to show that he had taken into consideration the factors that applied in their particular case when considering whether to do the works such as the views of the tenants and the financial impact on the tenants and that having taken into consideration these factors it was a reasonable to continue with his course of action. If so, it was likely that the costs had been reasonably incurred.

Radcliffe Investment Properties Ltd v Meeson [2023]

It was held that the cost of a waking watch had not been reasonably incurred to the extent the service costs charged were attributable to the landlord's failure to comply with its fire safety obligations. If the landlord had complied with its duty, the fire safety defects would have been discovered and the waking watch would not have been necessary.

Have the works/services been carried out to a reasonable standard?

The second part of the test for reasonableness is whether the works/services carried out by the landlord have been carried out to a reasonable standard. This will be for the Court/Tribunal to assess, and the tenant will need to provide evidence that the works were not sufficient. This will usually mean providing evidence that more works are needed to rectify the deficiencies in the work already done.

If it is found that the works are not to a reasonable standard, the Court/Tribunal will assess what costs the landlord is entitled to for the works taking into consideration any deficiencies. The fact the works were not carried to a reasonable standard will not mean that tenants can simply refuse to pay any of the costs. It will just be a matter of the Court to determine what proportion of the costs are still payable.

Relevant Case

Saunderson v Cambridge Park Court Residents Association Limited Re: Cambridge Park Court [2018]

There was a communal heating system, and the tenants were liable to pay the costs of these services under the service charge clause. One of the tenants installed their own boiler in their flat. As they were not receiving any benefit from the communal heating system, they objected to paying the service charges. It was held that as the landlord was not supplying any heating to the tenant's flat, it could not be seen that the landlord was providing the heating to a reasonable standard. The service charges were not due.

Can a landlord's delay in carrying out works be used to argue the costs claimed are unreasonable?

It is a common scenario that arises that the landlord has delayed carrying out works and complying with their obligations under the lease. As a result of the delay, the works required may have become more extensive than if they had been carried out the required works in a proper and timely manner and the more expensive works now being claimed from the tenants may have been avoided.

It seems unreasonable that the landlord can now claim costs for works where a substantial sum of those costs arises out of historical delay and the landlord's breach of covenant. However, If the proposed necessary works have increased due to the landlord having delayed the repairs, it does not mean that the greater amount of works is not reasonably incurred.

This seems unjust to the tenants, but tenants are able make a separate claim in damages against their landlord for breach of covenant. The tenant can also issue a counterclaim for damages in response to any claim issued by the landlord for recovery of the service charges. The number of damages caused by historic delay is hard to quantify and the tenant will ideally need an expert report that assesses what they believed the difference would have been if the works had been carried out when they should have been compared to now. There may also be previous quotes for the works before the property deteriorated further, which they landlord failed to implement, that may assist.

Any advance interim payments must be reasonable

Section 19(2) of the Act sets out that if the landlord is entitled to advance payments under the service charge clause, these payments must still be reasonable. The same section also sets out how a landlord should deal with any adjustments that are required when the actual expenditure is incurred, and the actual expenditure is more or less than the sums received from advance payments.

The provision for advance payments is fairly usual in a service charge clause as a landlord will not want to incur the expenditure out of their own pocket whilst seeking recovery of the sums due. The advance payments are based on what the landlord estimates the costs will be for the works/services, so it makes sense that the section also deals with what happens if the estimate was higher or lower than the actual costs. Section 19(2) does not impose a deadline for making these adjustments. However, it has been held that balancing payments should be paid within a reasonable time. In addition, the lease should be referred to as the service charge clause in the lease is likely to deal with this if it has been efficiently drafted.

When demanding further payments as a result of an underpayment for the services through advance payments, the landlord will need to comply with Section 20B of the Act (discussed below).

<u>Relevant Cases</u>

Knapper v Francis [2017]

A number of tenants under long leases at a holiday park had to make advance payments in respect of the management of the holiday park. The costs claimed included the costs of hiring a site manager and refurbishment of a play area. Works were carried out, but the landlord did not end up hiring a site manager or refurbishing the play area like they had first anticipated. It was held that the relevant date to determine reasonableness of the advance payment is the date the contractual liability to make the payment arose. At the time the landlord made the demand the landlord was intending to hire a site manager and do the refurbishment so contractually it was payable. However, the advance payments charged for these works that were not carried out did still need to be reasonable and the Court commented that matters not known by the landlord when they charged the sums due such as the fact, they could have employed a site managed for a lesser sum could be used to assess reasonableness. In this case it was found that the charges were reasonable, but it is important to note that matters not known to the landlord at the date the contractual liability arose can be used to assess reasonableness.

Avon Ground Rents Ltd v Cowley and others [2019]

The landlord was replacing a defective membrane that was allowing water penetration into the building. Under the lease, the landlord was entitled to advance payments for the works. The building was still under warranty and NHBC had indicated they would pay for the works. It has held that it was unreasonable for the landlord to request advance payments where the costs were recoverable from a third party.

<u>**Administration charges must be reasonable**</u>

Administration charges need to be reasonable pursuant to the Commonhold and Leasehold Reform Act 2002 (CLARA 2002).

Part 1 of Schedule 11 of the CLARA 2002 sets out the charges to which this is applied. They are in summary any amount payable by the tenant in addition to rent and in connection with the costs incurred in granting applications or approvals under the lease, the provision of documents or information and in respect of breaches of covenants in the lease.

On the one hand CLARA 2002 seems to only apply to variable administration charges and not those charges fixed by the lease. However, CLARA 2002 then goes on to state that the tenant can challenge fixed charges by applying to the tribunal to vary the lease on the basis that the fixed charges are not reasonable. Essentially therefore all administration charges can be subject to the reasonableness test, and it is something that practitioners should be aware of when drafting any fixed administration charges or formulas for assessing administration charges in the lease. It is better to try and ensure the fixed charges are reasonable at the drafting stage than incur the costs of a dispute further down the line.

Parties cannot apply to the Tribunal to assess reasonableness if the tenant has already agreed or admitted the sums due. If a tenant is unsure whether the administration charge is reasonable it is advised that if they do make payment, they state at the same time that they are making payment so that they are not in breach of the lease, but the charge is not agreed and they reserve their right to pursue the question of whether it is reasonable through the tribunal.

Summary

Sums charged to the tenants in respect of service charges including advance payments, administration charges and management fees have to be reasonable. The test for whether they are reasonable is a 2-part test as to whether they have been reasonably incurred and if the works/services are to a reasonable standard. If the charges are not reasonable, the landlord is unlikely to recover the full sums demanded.

CHAPTER EIGHT

SERVICE CHARGE DEMANDS

Introduction

The Act provides that for service charges to become payable, a valid service charge demand needs to have been served within 18 months of the landlord incurring the costs. This chapter aims to clarify what needs to be included within a service charge demand, the consequences of failing to comply with the Act and how errors in service charge demands may be rectified.

Section 48 of the Landlord and Tenant Act 1987 ('LTA 1987')

A notice pursuant to section 48 of the LTA 1987 must be served on the tenants of the building before the landlord serves any service charge demands. A section 48 notice sets out the landlord's address for service of notices in England and Wales. It is now common practice to include the landlord's address for service of notices in the lease itself. If provision is made in the lease it should refer to section 48 of the LTA 1987. If this is the case it is not necessary to serve an additional notice. If the landlord has acquired the lease by buying the freehold or leasehold, they will need to serve notice under section 48 unless the new name and address for service of notices has been supplied in the notice of assignment sent to the tenant. Again, it should explicitly refer to section 48 of the LTA 1987.

Until such a notice is served no service charges as well as any rent are due from the tenant. It is therefore an essential step to take as soon as a landlord acquires or leases a property. A further section 48 Notice also will need serving if there is a change of service address for the landlord.

Failure to do so will again result in the landlord being unable to recover service charges or rent.

The Requirements for a Service Charge Demand

To be valid a service charge demand must:

- Include the name and address of the landlord (section 47(1)(a) of the LTA 1987).
- Include a summary of the rights and obligations of the tenants in (section 21B of the Act)

Name and address of the landlord

This is self-explanatory. The landlord for the purposes of the LTA 1987 is the immediate landlord who is entitled to the possession of the property. One issue that does arise is if the landlord is abroad. If this is the case the service charge demand must also include an address in England and Wales at which a tenant can service notices on the landlord.

Summary of Rights and Obligations

Section 21B of the Act, as inserted by the CLARA 2002, requires any service charge demand to be accompanied by a summary of the rights and obligation of the tenants. The wording used must follow the wording set out in the Service Charges (Summary of Rights and Obligations, and Transitional Provision) (England) Regulations 2007 and the Service Charges (Summary of Rights and Obligations, and Transitional Provision) (Wales) Regulations 2007.

Regulation 3 provide that the summary of rights and obligations must:

- Be legible and in typewritten or printed form of at least a 10 point.

- Include the title "Service Charges — Summary of tenants' rights and obligations"

- Include the statement set out at regulation 3(b).

In addition, the summary of rights and obligations should be on a separate sheet of paper that accompanies the service charge demand. Sending a summary of rights and obligations separate to the service charge demand is not sufficient and will invalidate the demand. This was held in the case of *Tingdene Holiday Parks Ltd v Cox [2011].*

If the Service Charge Demand does not meet the statutory requirements, any service charge or administration charge included in the demand is not due until the landlord has served the correct form of demand (*section 47(2), LTA 1987*). The landlord would also not be able to claim interest on any amount claimed in a defective demand until the error in the demand has been rectified. Rectification of service charge demands is discussed further below.

If the tenant pays the service charge demanded under an invalid service charge demand the tenant cannot require repayment.

<u>Relevant Case</u>

Middleton & Another v Karbon Homes Ltd (2023)

It was held that if a landlord fails to include the required statutory information in a service charge demand, the service charge is not payable until the omission is put right. However, if the tenant complies with the relevant demand and pays the service charge, section 21B does not give the tenant the right to require repayment.

When must the service charge demand be served?

Section 20B of the Act states that a landlord must issue the service charge demand within 18 months of the costs being incurred. If the demand is provided after 18 months, the landlord will not be able to recover the costs claimed, unless the landlord served a notice is served during the 18 months stating that costs have been incurred and that the tenant would subsequently be required to contribute to them by payment of a service charge.

Relevant Cases

Gilje v Charlegrove Securities Ltd [2003]

It was held that section 20B was not relevant if all of the following apply:

- Payments on accounts had been made in respect of the service charges
- The landlord's actual expenditure does not exceed the payments on account.
- No request for further payment needed to be made by the landlord.

This finding was based on the fact that the purpose of Section 20(B) was to protect tenants from unexpected expenditure not to prevent a landlord from recovering sums due, of which the tenants had already had notice.

Holding & Management (Solitaire) Ltd v Sherwin [2010]

It was held that Section 20B is applicable if the landlord makes demands for balancing charges which relate to costs that were incurred more than 18 months previously.

This case dealt with whether the 18-month time limit runs from when an invoice was raised to the landlord for the supply of gas or when payment was made by the landlord. It was held that the 18-month time limit runs from the date the liability is properly invoiced rather than the date that service was obtained. However, this is not set in stone and an analysis of the facts is required to assess if this is applicable. This case was quite unusual as several years had passed since the gas had been supplied before the landlord served a service charge demand. The delay was due to the fact that the services were invoiced by the wrong company. When the correct company invoiced the landlord, and the landlord paid the tenant argued the landlord was out of time.

Skelton v DBS Homes (Kings Hill) Ltd [2017]

The tenants sought determination from the tribunal that the service charges were not payable as they had not been demanded in accordance with the lease. The lease provisions were not clearly drafted but seemed to state that the landlord needed to serve a statement of the service charges on the tenant for each upcoming service charge year. The estimate was to include a statement showing the service charges payable in 2 equal instalments on account of the proposed expenditure. The landlord served the statements on each year, but it was not accompanied by an estimate. The tenant claimed the service charges were not payable as the landlord had failed to serve a valid demand within 18 months. The landlord claimed that the time limit did not apply because the service charge demand was for an on-account service charge. The Court of Appeal held that the 18-month time limit applied to service charges in respect of costs to be incurred as well as costs that have been incurred. This case was distinguished from *Gilje v Charlegrove Securities Ltd [2003]* on the basis that in that case the service charge demand for payment was made before, not after, the landlord had incurred the costs.

Administration Charge Demands

The provisions of section 47 and 48 of the LTA 1987 also apply to demands for administration charges.

Schedule 11 of CLARA 2002 sets out that demands for payment for administration charge also must be accompanied by a summary of rights and obligations. The requirements for this summary are set out in the Administration Charges (Summary of Rights and Obligations) (England) Regulations 2007 and the Administration Charges (Summary of Rights and Obligations) (Wales) Regulations 2007.

Regulation 2 provides that the summary of rights and obligations must:

- Be legible and in typewritten or printed form of at least a 10 point.
- Include the title "Service Charges — Summary of tenants' rights and obligations"
- Include the statement set out at regulation 2(b)

Until a demand for the administration charges meets these requirements, the charges will not be payable.

Amending errors in service charge demands

If the landlord has made an error in their service charge demand, they can still serve an amended service charge demand. If a tenant is disputing payment only on the grounds that the service charge demand is deficient, they should be aware that even if the service charge demand is invalid, they are still ultimately likely to be liable to pay the sums due when an amended version is served.

Relevant Cases

Tingdene Holiday Parks Ltd v Cox and Others [2011]

The landlord failed to attach a summary of the rights and obligations to the service charge demand as required under section 21B of the Act. A further demand was issued that was accompanied by a summary. It was held this rectified the defect and the service charges were payable.

Johnson v County Bideford Ltd [2012]

The service charge demand was invalid pursuant to section 47 of the LTA 1987 because the name and address of the managing agent had been included on the demand instead of the landlord's name and address. It was held that this error could be corrected, and this correction could have retrospective effect.

Summary

It is crucial that a landlord considers the legislation when serving service charge demands. A failure to do so or comply will result in the charges not being payable until a valid demand is served. This can be particularly detrimental if the landlord is close to the 18-month time limit to demand the charges.

CHAPTER NINE

THE RIGHT TO REQUEST INFORMATION RELATING TO SERVICE CHARGES

Introduction

Tenants are entitled to request information from the landlord in relation to the service charges being made. Their statutory rights are as follows:

- To seek a summary of the service charge account
- To inspect accounts, receipts and other documents relating to the service charge summary and to take copies of these
- To request a summary of insurance cover and to inspect insurance policy documents

This chapter summarises these rights and the consequences for the landlord in not complying.

Section 21 of the Act – Request for a written summary of costs

Usually there is a clause in the lease that provides for the landlord to provide a statement of account. Practitioners should review this initially. In addition to the rights in the lease tenants can seek a summary of the costs incurred in the last service charge year or in the last 12 months pursuant to section 21 of the Act. Any request should be writing.

Section 21 (4) of the Act states that once a request has been made the landlord needs to reply within the later of 1 month from the request or

Six months after the end of the period referred to in section 21(1)(a) or (b) of the Act.

Section 21 (5) states that the summary must include the following:

- How the costs have been or will be reflected in demands for service charges.
- State whether any of the costs relate to works which are grant aided.
- Summarise costs in relation to matters where no demand for payment has been received by the landlord, matters where a demand for payment has been received but payment has not been made and matters where a demand for payment has been made and received.
- Specify the total amount the landlord has receive don account of service charges and the amount that which remains to the credit of the tenants.

The summaries of the costs are for the applicable 12-month period and in the case of 4 or more tenants being liable to pay the charges, the summary must be certified by a qualified accountant. The requirements for that certification are set out at section 21(5) and (5) of the Act.

As an aside, in respect of grant aided works, section 20A (1) of the Act prevents the inclusion of costs of works in the service charge if the landlord receives a grant in respect of those works.

Section 22 – Request for further information

Tenants also have a right under section 22 of the Act to request reasonable facilities to inspect and copy accounts, receipts or other documents relevant to the statement of account. This request must be made within 12 months of the end of the relevant accounting period or within 6 months of receiving the summary under section 21 of the Act.

Once a section 22 request is received, the landlord has one month to comply and the right to inspect and take copies need to be available for at least 2 months. The facilities to inspect the documents should be made free of charge. However, a landlord may be able to recover these costs under management costs in the lease. The landlord is entitled to make reasonable charges in respect of taking copies of the relevant documents.

Service charges levied by superior landlords

If the landlord who receives a section 21 or section 22 request is an intermediate landlord, they can request the information from the superior landlord under section 23 of the Act who then must comply within a reasonable time.

Failing to comply with tenant's requests under sections 21-23 of the Act

It is a summary offence for the landlord to fail to perform their obligations under section 21-23 of the Act, without reasonable excuse. The landlord will therefore be liable to a fine not exceeding level 4 on the standard scale.

Summary

If a request is received from a tenant pursuant to section 21 -23 of the Act, the landlord should ensure they immediately familiarise themselves with both what they need to do to comply and also the time limits to respond to ensure they avoid the consequences of failing to do so.

CHAPTER TEN

OTHER STATUTORY RESTRICTIONS IN RESPECT OF RESIDENTIAL SERVICE CHARGES

Introduction

There are a number of miscellaneous statutory restrictions imposed in respect of residential service charges which practitioners should be aware of in case it is applicable. These are detailed briefly below.

The Building Safety Act 2022

The Building Safety Act 2022 ('the BSA 2022') prevents landlords of relevant buildings of a certain height from being able to recover costs for certain building safety remediation works through service charges from qualifying tenants. This forces landlords to seek alternative funding for such works, such as government grants or contributions from developers. Qualifying tenants who have already paid for building safety remediation works may also be able to apply for a refund through an Remediation Contribution Order. The BSA 2022 is a complex piece of legislation and many provisions of the BSA 2022 are unclear and are still being interpreted through the Courts. A detailed analysis of the BSA 2022 is beyond the scope of this book. If the building Is at least 11 metres high or has 5 storeys, Landlords and Managing Agents should review If the works to be carried out fall within the BSA 2022 and if so, if they are recoverable a service charges. Landlords and Managing agents should also be aware that if any works have previously been carried out that fall within the BSA 2022 they may be subject to an application for refund.

Leases with a term of less than 7 years

Usually, landlords are recovering service charges in respect of long leases. If the landlord is claiming service charges in respect of a residential tenancy of under 7 years, the landlord is unable to claim for works which they are obliged to do under section 11 of the Act. Section 11 of the Act imposes an obligation on the landlord to:

- keep in repair the structure and exterior of the dwelling (including drains, external pipes, gutters and external windows).

- keep in repair and proper working order the installations in the dwelling for the supply of water, gas and electricity and for sanitation (including basins, sinks, baths and sanitary conveniences); and

- keep in repair and proper working order the installations in the dwelling for space heating and heating water.

A landlord cannot contract out of section 11 in respect of these shorter leases and as such cannot seek to recoup the costs of doing these works from the tenants.

The right to buy process

The grant of long shared ownership leases under the right to buy legislation is governed by section 143 onwards of the Housing Act 1985. If the right to buy process applies the landlord must serve notice on the tenant. The requirements of this notice are set out at section 125 of the Housing Act 1985. Section 125 also limits the tenant's liability in respect of costs incurred on repairs or improvements during the initial period to the estimated costs set out in the notice, together with an allowance for inflation.

Trusts of Service Charge Payments

Any contributions to service charges received from the tenants must be held on trust pursuant to section 42 of the LTA 1987. This is the case even if there is only one contributing tenant and applies to all funds to which section 18 of the Act applies and to all landlords that are not exempt under section 58 of the LTA 1987. The section also applies to any investments or income relating to the sums received. The funds can only be used to meet the costs for which the service charges were payable.

Management of Residential leasehold property

The management of residential property and right to manage companies is outside the remit of this book but for the standards of management reference should be made to the RICS Service Charge Residential Management Case (3rd Edition). Compliance with the code is not compulsory but a breach of the code can be used as evidence in court proceedings. There are also rules on the procedure for replacement of managing agents which is detailed under section 24 of the LTA 1987 and consultation rules in respect of the appointment of managing agents at section 30B of the Act.

Mixed use premises

Where service charges are payable in respect of mixed-use premises landlords need to comply with the more stringent residential procedures. This applies even if the residential tenant is an under-tenant.

Relevant Cases

Heron Maple House Ltd v Central Estate Ltd [2002]

The building was divided into commercial and residential premises. The landlord did not carry out a section 20 consultation. It was established that section 20 applies where a property includes any let residential unit.

Oakfern Properties Limited v Desmond Ruddy [2006]

Established further that a residential occupier in mixed use premises can directly challenge service charges raised by the superior landlord based on non-compliance with the consultation requirements.

Summary

The above is a brief overview of matters that may need to be considered when dealing with service charge disputes. Whether they are applicable will obviously depend on the facts of the case.

PART THREE

DISPUTES AND REMEDIES

Part 1 and 2 have dealt with the interpretation of service charge clauses as well as the statutory obligations that are relevant in of service charges in the residential sector. The next logical question is how to deal with non-compliance on the part of the landlord or failure to pay on the part of the tenant. Part 3 aims to take practitioners through the various options of how to deal with service charge disputes together with the advantages and disadvantages of each option.

CHAPTER ELEVEN

ALTERNATIVE DISPUTE RESOLUTION

Introduction

The first thing to check when reviewing a service charge dispute is whether the lease provides for provision for disputes to be referred to an arbitrator or expert in the first instance. If so, the parties need to comply with this requirement. Even if it is not provided for in the lease, the parties may still want to consider ADR before going down the tribunal or Court route. This chapter sets out a brief description of a few ADR options to help decide which avenue may be appropriate in each particular case.

ADR Procedures

There are several advantages to going down the ADR route as opposed to the Court. It is a lot more cost effective and usually leads to a quicker resolution. It is also a lot more flexible. The usual ADR procedures used are mediation, independent expert determination and arbitration.

Mediation

A mediation involves a third party that is unconnected to the dispute and therefore neutral. The aim of the arbitrator is to help the parties reach an agreement without giving their personal opinion. The third party will ask the parties to explain and clarify their positions. Usually there will be a meeting with all the parties and the mediator present at the beginning of the mediation, but mediation can take place with both parties remaining in separate rooms throughout if required. A good mediator will be able to suggest ways forward and possible satisfactory solutions. Mediation is unlikely to work if the parties are not willing to enter into a dialogue, negotiate and move from their starting position.

Independent expert determination

This is a process by which an independent third-party acts as an expert in the field rather than a judge or arbitrator. The parties can agree the expert to be appointed or refer it to an appointing body such as the CIArb. The expert will hear evidence from both parties and then makes a decision which is binding. The decision is confidential.

Arbitration

This is a more formal procedure which is similar to Court proceedings. The parties can agree who to appoint or apply for one to be appointed. The arbitrator will set directions for submissions and evidence. The arbitrator will then make an award which binds the parties. The parties can apply to Court to enforce the award if the parties fail to comply with the contents. Although more formal, arbitration is a lot more flexible than court proceedings and at less cost.

Summary

Settling a matter through ADR is a much more appealing option for both landlords and tenants. In addition, if one party does offer ADR, it is expected that the other party will accept this offer. Failure to do so could lead to cost consequences if the matter proceeds to trial.

CHAPTER TWELVE

APPLYING TO VARY THE LEASE

Introduction

Section 35 and section 37 of the LTA 1987 provides that a party to a long lease can apply to the Tribunal to vary the lease. This may be an applicable remedy if it can be shown that the lease fails to make satisfactory provision for recovery of computation of service charges. The procedure and matters that a party should consider when considering this application are detailed below.

What is a long lease?

A long lease (a lease over 21 years) shall not be regarded as a long lease of a flat if (a) the demised premises consist of or include three or more flats contained in the same building; or (b) the lease constitutes a tenancy to which Part II of the Landlord and Tenant Act 1954 applies.

Satisfactory Provision

Under section 35 the application for variation is in respect of just one lease and must be on the basis that the lease fails to make satisfactory provision for one or more of the matters at section 35(2)(a) -(f) of the LTA 1987. Section 35 (e) and (f) are the sections applicable to service charges and are as follows:

(e) the recovery of one party to the lease from another party to it of expenditure incurred by him, or on his behalf, for the benefit of that other party or of a number of persons who include that other party: or

(f) the computation of a service charges under the lease.

Section 35(4) of the LTA 1987 states that a lease fails to make "satisfactory" provision in respect of section 35(f) the calculation of the service charge due under a lease, if all the following conditions are satisfied:

- The lease provides that the service charge is to be a proportion of the landlord's expenditure.
- The other tenants of the building are liable under their leases to pay a proportion of the landlord's expenditure.
- The combined total of the service charge proportions either exceeds or is less than the landlord's total expenditure.

The power of the Tribunal to vary the service charge clause is discretionary. Section 38(6) provides that the Tribunal should not make a variation order if it is likely that the variation will prejudice the respondent to the application, any person not party to the application, where an award for compensation would not be appropriate or if the Tribunal thinks for any other reason that it would not be reasonable to do so. If a variation order is made, the Tribunal may also make an order for compensation to any party they believe may suffer a loss as a result.

Section 37 of the LTA 1987 sets out the procedure for an application for the variation of 2 or more leases.

Where a variation order is made it will take effect from the date the order is made or a later date if specified in the order.

Relevant Cases

Triplerose Ltd v Stride [2019]

Triperlose's lease did not require them to contribute to the costs of repair and maintenance of the building. The other 3 leases in the building did contain provision to contribute. Triperlose applied to the Tribunal for determination as to whether service charges were payable. In response the landlord sought a variation of the lease. On appeal the requested variation of the lease was refused on the basis that they had not satisfied section 35. The fact the lease was different to others in the building did not automatically make the lease terms unsatisfactory. The landlord had not provided any evidence to support their assertion that the terms were unsatisfactory or had caused any problems. The building was in a reasonable condition and the other 3 flats had been covering the shortfall.

London Borough of Camden v Morath and others [2019]

The London Borough of Camden was liable under their headlease to pay 25% of costs incurred in repair of Brunswick Centre. The premises were sublet under 3 different types of subleases. One of the types of subleases did not contain provision for the sub tenant to pay a proportionate part of what Camden paid toward the head lessor's expenditure. Camden applied to vary the terms of this type of sub lease under section 35 of the LTA 1987. The application was unsuccessful. The Tribunal held that the lease wording was clear and workable. The lease had made satisfactory provision and it was not for the Tribunal to vary a lease so that it was the same as the other sub leases granted.

Summary

If a party is likely to be successful in an application to vary the lease they need to have clear evidence that the current terms are unsatisfactory. A variation order is not going to be granted simply because a party would prefer a lease to be worded differently to assist for example with the recovery of service charges.

CHAPTER THIRTEEN

APPLICATIONS FOR DETERMINATION AS TO WHETHER SERVICE CHARGES ARE PAYABLE

Introduction

The usual route for a range of residential service charge disputes is to apply to the FTT for determination. The number of residential service charge disputes issued in the Tribunal has been increasing each year. Applications are fairly easy to complete with the application form available online.

What can be determined by the FTT?

It has been held that the FTT can determine the following: -

- Whether the service charge is payable under the terms of the lease.
- Whether the service charge has been reasonably incurred –Even if consultation has been carried out, it doesn't mean that the service charge is automatically payable. It is still subject to Section 18 unreasonableness.
- By whom and to whom the service charge is payable.
- The date on which the service charge may be payable.

- The manner of payment i.e., if it is to be paid by direct debit or standing order.

- Whether the consultation procedure has been correctly followed and if not, a dispensation should be given.

The procedure

After issuing an application, the matter will be listed for directions. After the directions have been complied with, the FTT will send out a written decision and reasons for it within 6 weeks of the hearing (or proper determination if no hearing). In some circumstances, the FTT will inform you of the outcome at the end of the hearing itself. This is quite rare and usually more simple matters.

Relevant Case

The Garden Quarter (Caversfield) Management Company Ltd v Ortet [2025]

The Right to Manage Company ('the RTM') carried out works to the building which included paintwork. The RTM charged the leaseholders for the costs. One of the tenants applied to the First Tier Tribunal to dispute the costs on the basis that the works undertaken were of a poor quality.

The First Tier Tribunal found that only £1,000 of the demanded amount should be payable by the tenants. The RTM appealed the decision stating that the FTT did not sufficiently explain its findings or provide rationale in its decision.

The Upper Tribunal stated that the First Tier Tribunal is required to clearly explain its decision when determining the payability and quantity of service charges. The FTT had inadequately explained its decision and failed to address the issues including the timing of the service charge demand and the issues raised by the leaseholders regarding the quality of work. The case was remitted back to the FTT for a further decision.

Application for a declaration

The other route a party may go down is to apply for a declaration. A Landlord could apply to the court for a declaration on the true interpretation of the lease/correctness of service charge certificate/calculation etc. It's possible for a landlord to apply for a declaration before incurring the costs. This has been encouraged in a number of cases and seems an appropriate route when the landlord is unsure if he is covered for the works he is intending to carry out for example, in a sweeper clause. If a landlord simply goes ahead with works that they are unsure are covered by the service charge clause, they risk a dispute from the tenants regarding liability and ultimately the risk that the service charges will not be payable. This could leave a landlord or a managing company in a very difficult position financially.

Relevant case

Reston Limited v Hudson [1990]

In this case the landlord proposed to replace all of the window frames in a block of flats. However, not all of them were in disrepair at the time. It made sense for the landlord to carry out repairs on the window frames of the whole block. The other windows were likely to fall into disrepair shortly and to carry out the repair in bulk would be cheaper than in 2 or more occasions. The landlord was concerned that they might not be able to recover the sums incurred if not all the windows were in disrepair so they applied to the tribunal to determine if the tenants would be liable for the full sums. It was held that the landlord could replace all of the window frames and recover the full costs incurred from the tenants.

Summary

The FTT have the jurisdiction to deal with a lot of the common issues that arise with residential service charges and an application to the FTT is likely to be preferable to the Court if the dispute if in one of these areas. Landlords should also carefully consider issuing a claim for a declaration that particular service charges are payable if the wording in the lease is unclear to prevent possible financial loss if they are not recoverable.

CHAPTER FOURTEEN

TENANTS REMEDIES FOR NON-PERFORMANCE OF THE LANDLORD'S OBLIGATIONS

Introduction

The landlord's obligations under the legislation to enable them to claim service charges have been discussed at length. However, what happens if the landlord just fails to carry out the repairs they are obliged to do under the lease and what can the tenant do in those circumstances? This chapter sets out the possible options available to tenants.

Application for an injunction to force the landlord to carry out works

To proceed down this avenue there needs to be an urgency to the works, or the disrepair needs to be very severe. It is only advisable in exceptional circumstances as the tenant is asking the Court to order an interim injunction in the first instance. A Court will need to determine if this is applicable without the matter being fully argued at Trial. The tenant would need to have significant evidence including a surveyor's report or expert evidence showing the works are needed immediately. If an interim injunction is granted the matter will then be listed for directions and a hearing to decide a final injunction should be ordered.

Issue a claim for damages

The tenant can issue a claim for damages resulting from the landlord's failure to repair. Prior to issuing proceedings, the tenant will need to have contacted the landlord and given them a reasonable time to comply with their covenants. The losses claimed must be reasonably foreseeable and compensation will only be payable from the date on which the Landlord had knowledge of disrepair. The amount awarded will depend on the losses that have actually been suffered.

Summary

A tenant should only consider the first option in severe circumstances. In both instances the tenant should have approached the landlord to do the works and given them reasonable time to do so. What is reasonable obviously depends on the urgency of the works.

CHAPTER FIFTEEN

LANDLORD'S REMEDIES FOR NON-PAYMENT OF SERVICE CHARGES

Introduction

If the tenant has failed to pay the service charges and it is not applicable to apply to the tribunal for determination that they are payable, the landlord needs to be able to enforce the right to recover the sums due. The landlord is no longer able to distain for service charges which are reserved as rent under the lease as this was abolished as from 6 April 2014. The landlord does however have recourse through the Courts for recovery of the sums due either through issuing forfeiture proceedings or a debt claim.

Forfeiture of the lease

Residential property is subject to a number of restrictions in respect of forfeiting for service charges and administration charges as follows:

- The landlord cannot forfeit the lease unless the amount of service charge has been agreed or admitted by the tenant or has been determined at least 14 clear days previously by a Court or a tribunal (section 84(1) and (2) Housing Act 1996)

- A landlord is prohibited from service of a forfeiture notice which is a long lease (granted for a term of over 21 years) if the tenant has not admitted the breach of covenant and the landlord has not obtained a Court or a tribunal final determination that the tenant is in breach of covenant (section 168 of the CLARA 2002)

- If 1/2 above applies, the landlord must first serve the tenant with a Section 146 Notice specifying the default and requiring the tenant to pay within a reasonable time. Reasonable time is normally deemed to be around 14 days. The Notice must also state that Section 81 of the Housing Act applies and set out the effect of section 81(1).

- Forfeiture is not permitted for small amounts of arrears or where there is only a short period of delay in making payment. The minimum amount of arrears on which forfeiture can be based is currently £250.00 and the minimum period of delayed payment is currently 3 years (section 167 of the CLARA 2002)

Even if the above applies a possession order will need to be obtained to get possession from the tenant and the landlords needs to be mindful of the Protection from Eviction Act 1977. The tenant is also likely to get relief from forfeiture if they pay the sums due within a reasonable time and automatically if they pay the arrears 5 clear working days before any substantive possession hearing.

Issue court proceedings for recovery of the service charge arrears

Service charges will only become due once all the procedures have been correctly followed in respect of consultation and service charge demands and any obligations under the lease have been complied with regarding payment of the arrears.

Relevant cases

Canary Riverside PTE Ltd v Schilling [2005]

The lease provided that the landlord had to give the tenant written notice of any revised estimate of the annual service costs if it exceeded the previously notified estimate. The landlord incurred significant costs above their initial estimate and claimed the additional costs without providing the revised estimate. It was held that the landlord could not recover the additional sums incurred as they had failed to comply with the procedure in the lease.

Warrior Quay Management Company Limited v Joachim [2008]

The lease provided that the landlord was to provide audited accounts in order for the tenants to be liable for any balancing charges. The landlord failed to provide the audited accounts and issued proceedings. It was held that the landlord could not issue for recovery of the charges until such time as they had complied with the requirements under the lease and served the audited accounts.

Once the landlord has complied with any preconditions in the lease, it is advisable that the landlord then serves a letter before action on the tenant providing them with 30 days to reply to the Claim. This is more essential if the landlord is a company and is acting against an individual. If no response is received on the expiry of the letter before action or matters do not progress after the initial response the landlord can then issue proceedings. There will be Court issue fee payable, the sum of which will depend on the value of the claim. Once the claim has been issued and served the tenant will have 14 days to file and acknowledgment of service as with any debt claim. If the tenant fails to do so or fails to file a defence 14 days after the acknowledgment of service, the landlord can request judgment. If the tenant does file a defence, the Court will list the case for directions and a trial. If a defence is filed, the proceedings will become very lengthy and costly.

Once a judgement is obtained it is a matter of considering how the landlord can enforce. This is where the tenant's financial situation is key. If the tenant does not have the funds to pay the judgment it may be that the landlord will be throwing good money after bad in trying to recoup the same. However, in most cases, I would expect the tenant to at least have a leasehold interest which a landlord could consider obtaining a charge over for the sums due. The other routes a landlord may consider are serving a statutory demand on the tenant (if the sums due are over £5,000), a warrant of execution or an attachment of earnings. The best method of enforcement will depend on the circumstances of the case, and it may be worthwhile instructing an enquiry agent to carry out an asset sweep on the tenant in the first instance to assist in deciding the best method of enforcement.

Commerz Real Investment gesellschaft MBH v TFS Stores Ltd [2021]

It was held that a landlord was entitled to summary judgement against its tenant for non-payment of rent and service charges during the COVID-19 pandemic.

Summary

Forfeiture of a residential lease on the basis of non-payment of service charges is not an easy process and will not always be applicable. The legislation has made it difficult to forfeit the lease because the tenants will most likely be losing a long-term interest in their lease. The best option in the first instance may therefore be to issue a debt claim in the hope this puts enough pressure on the tenant to pay if indeed they do have the funds to pay.

CHAPTER SIXTEEN

LEGAL COSTS

Introduction

If the landlord issues proceedings for arrears of service charge through the Court and obtains a judgment, the usual position is that the landlord will be awarded costs from the tenant. Costs are usually awarded on a standard basis and less than the actual costs incurred. However, this is not the case in small claims matters where each party will bear their own costs and in respect of Tribunal proceedings, the usual position is that each party bears their own costs. There can be come variation from this position though and the wording of the lease can also be relevant.

Costs in the Tribunal

As stated above the usual position is each party bears their own costs. Rule 13 of the Tribunal Procedure (First Tier Tribunal) (Property Chamber) Rules 2013 sets out that a Tribunal may make an order for costs only "if a person has acted unreasonably in brining, defending or conducting proceedings". Reference should also be made to Schedule 12 of CLARA 2002.

Despite the above, the wording of the lease may allow the recovery of legal costs. Schedule 12 of CLARA 2002 does not restrict a contractual right to costs.

Applications by the tenant

Section 20C of the Act provides that a tenant may apply to the tribunal for an order (section 20C direction) that:

> *"All or any of the costs incurred, or to be incurred, by the landlord in connection with proceedings before a court, residential property tribunal or leasehold valuation tribunal, or the Upper Tribunal, or in connection with arbitration proceedings, are not to be regarded as relevant costs to be taken into account in determining the amount of any service charge payable by the tenant."*

A tenant can also make an application under paragraph 5A of Schedule 11 of CLARA 2020 to limit the landlord's recovery of litigation costs as an administration charge. The tenant can apply for a determination under this Schedule in respect of costs yet to be incurred or already incurred.

Recovery of costs

The recovery of legal costs through the court or tribunal is not clear cut is ultimately usually down to the discretion of the court or tribunal and what they consider to be just and equitable in the circumstances. To assist in understanding the recovery of legal costs some cases are detailed below.

Relevant cases

Sella House Ltd v Mears [1989]

The lease allowed the recovery through the service charges of the costs of collecting the rent and employing professional persons for the administration of the building. The landlord argued that this covered his legal costs. It was held that the wording of the service charge clause should be clear and unambiguous to allow recovery of legal costs. This clause did not specifically provide for legal costs and they were not recoverable.

Thanet Lodge RTM Company Ltd v Arun Mirchandani [2024]

This case dealt with a range of different legal costs and whether they were recoverable under the lease. It was held that the legal costs incurred relating to the constitution and management of the RTM were not recoverable as the right to manage legislation did not exist at the time the leases were executed and as such the cost in relation to this benefited only some of the leaseholders. In respect of the dispute resolution costs, whilst the wording of these particular leases may include legal advice, the absence of specific mention of legal costs combined with the context and purpose of the clause meant they were not payable. The wording of the service charge clause must be read in context and does not override the specific limitations in the lease. The parties would not have intended to impose uncertain and potentially significant legal costs as service charges without explicit wording.

Iperion Investments Corporation v Broadwalk House Residents Ltd [1995]

The lease provided for payment of:

> *"All costs ... properly incurred by the Landlord in carrying out its obligations ... under the covenants and conditions contained in the Head Lease ... and in the proper and reasonable management of [the property]."*

The Court of Appeal held that under this clause the landlord could recover the legal costs incurred as a result of managing the property.

Plantation Wharf Management Company Ltd v Jackson and another [2011]

The lease permitted the recovery of professional advisers' fees relating to the enforcement of covenants. It was held that the management company could recover its legal costs through the service charge, despite the fact the clause did not explicitly include the words "legal costs". This case illustrates that the absence of an express reference may not be fatal to the recovery of legal costs. The case also commented that when asked by a tenant to make a section 20 direction, the risk of a management company becoming insolvent is a relevant consideration.

Shearbarn Holiday Park Ltd v Wornell and others [2021]

A court order stated there was to be no order as to costs. The service charge clause in the lease stated that litigation costs could be recovered. It was held that the provision for recovery in the lease was overridden by the provision in the consent order stating there was to be no order as to costs. Whether this is the case in other matters, however, is going to be highly dependent on the facts of a particular case and the background to the consent order.

Criterion Buildings Ltd v McKinsey & Company Inc (United Kingdom) and another [2021]

The landlord was successful in obtaining judgment against the tenant for unpaid service charges. The Court then had to consider how to deal with costs. There was provision in the lease and supplemental lease that the tenant was to pay landlord's expenses "properly incurred" and "all costs, charges and expenses which the landlord may from time to time incur ...". It was held that the covenants in the lease and supplemental lease justified an order for the landlord's costs of the proceedings to be recovered as service charges and to be assessed on the indemnity basis.

Summary

There is no clear position on costs and whether costs are likely to be recovered will depend on an assessment of the wording of the relevant clauses in the lease and whether action is being taken through the Court or the Tribunal. In most cases the parties should be aware that there is a significant chance that they will have to bear their own costs even if they are successful.

CHAPTER SEVENTEEN

POSSIBLE FORTCOMING CHANGES TO THE LEGISLATION

This book has aimed to provide you with guidance on the current key statutory controls on residential service charges and the factors to consider when assessing residential service charge disputes. Residential service charges are a huge area and I have tried to focus on the areas that I see more frequently in my practice and that are prevalent in service charge disputes. Hopefully the contents will assist as a starting point in any disputes or on any review of service charge documents. It is a constantly changing area as can be seen from the case law provided and with the current number of disputes, I am sure there will be many more cases to report shortly.

In respect of the legislation, the Leasehold and Freehold Reform Act 2024 (LFRA 2024), was granted Royal Assent on 24 March 2024. This will make some significant changes to the law surrounding residential service charges but the majority of the relevant provisions have not yet been brought into force.

The proposed changes are as follows:

- The Act will be amended to include protections for tenants in respect of fixed service charges as well as variable service charges.

- Service charge demands must use a new, specified form that contains more detailed information.

- A future service charge demand notice must be given to tenants within 18 months of costs being incurred in order that those costs can be subsequently recovered.

- For certain variable service charges, landlords must give tenants within six months of the end of the 12-month accounting period a statement of account in a specified form and a written report about the statement prepared by a qualified accountant.

- For fixed and variable service charges, landlords must give tenants a service charge report within one month of the end of the 12-month accounting period in respect of service charges arising in that period.

- Tenants will have an enhanced right to request copies of documents related to service charges, insurance, and management, including up to six years of historical data.

- Certain insurance costs connected with arranging or managing insurance will be prohibited from inclusion in a variable service charge.

- Landlords will be required to publish an administration charge schedule. This should specify the amount of each charge. Administration charges will be payable only to the extent the amount, or details of how the amount will be determined, appear on this published administration charge schedule for 28 days ending on the date of demand.

- The presumption that tenants must pay their landlord's legal costs in a dispute will be removed. Instead, landlords will need to apply to a tribunal to recover these costs, and tenants will have the right to ask the tribunal to order the landlord to pay their legal costs.

- A landlord's recovery of non-litigation costs in connection with enfranchisement, lease extension or Right to Manage claims through a variable service charge will be prohibited. Provisions in leases or other agreements that permit recovery of these costs will not be enforceable. This is already in force in respect of Right to claims.

We can only wait to see when and how the above new legislation will be implemented in due course.

MORE BOOKS BY LAW BRIEF PUBLISHING

A selection of our other titles available now:-

'A Practical Guide to Probation Breaches and Other Applications' by Mark Thomas

'A Practical Guide to Remarriage and Divorce' by Cordelia Williams & Claire Howard

'A Practical Guide to Privacy, Transparency, Reporting Restrictions and Closed Proceedings in the Court of Protection' by Laura Mannering

'Beaumont on Barristers – A Guide to Defending Disciplinary Proceedings (Second Edition)' by Marc Beaumont

'A Practical Guide to Payments for Environmental Services' by Ben Sharples

'A Practical Guide to the Law of Pregnancy and Maternity at Work' by Rebecca Thomas

'A Practical Guide to Redundancy – Second Edition' by Philip Hyland & Collette Moore

'A Practical Guide to International Issues for Scottish Family Lawyers' by Susie Mountain, Donna McKay, Ken MacDonald

'A Practical Guide to the Law on Deprivation of Liberty' by Ben Troke

'A Practical Guide to Rights over Airspace and Subsoil – Second Edition' by Daniel Gatty

'A Practical Guide to the Law in Relation to Inquests' by Ramya Nagesh

'A Practical Guide to the Construction and Rectification of Wills and Trust Instruments (Second Edition)' by Edward Hewitt

'A Practical Guide to Data Protection in Social Housing' by Clare Paterson

'A Practical Guide to Spousal Maintenance – Second Edition' by Liz Cowell

'A Practical Guide to International Parental Child Abduction Law (England and Wales)' by Dr Onyója Momoh

'A Practical Guide to Deprivation of British Citizenship' by Sean Ell

'A Practical Guide to Commercial Property Service Charges' by Rachel Garton

'A Practical Guide to Clinical Negligence – Third Edition' by Geoffrey Simpson-Scott (Geoff)

'A Practical Guide to the Rights of Grandparents in Children Proceedings – Second Edition' by Stuart Barlow

'The Electronic Communications Code: A Practical Guide – Second Edition' by Kerry Bretherton KC, James Castle, Mark Loveday
'A Practical Guide to the Independent School Standards – September 2023 Edition' by Sarah McKimm
'A Practical Guide to Estate Administration and Crypto Assets' by Richard Marshall
'A Practical Guide to Parental Alienation in Private and Public Law Children Cases' by Sam King QC & Frankie Shama
'Contested Heritage – Removing Art from Land and Historic Buildings' by Richard Harwood QC, Catherine Dobson, David Sawtell
'The Limits of Separate Legal Personality: When Those Running a Company Can Be Held Personally Liable for Losses Caused to Third Parties Outside of the Company' by Dr Mike Wilkinson
'A Practical Guide to Transgender Law' by Robin Moira White & Nicola Newbegin
'A Practical Guide to 'Stranded Spouses' in Family Law' by Mani Singh Basi
'A Practical Guide to Residential Freehold Conveyancing' by Lorraine Richardson
'A Practical Guide to Pensions on Divorce for Lawyers' by Bryan Scant
'A Practical Guide to Challenging Sham Marriage Allegations in Immigration Law' by Priya Solanki
'A Practical Guide to Digital Communications Evidence in Criminal Law' by Sam Willis
'A Practical Guide to Legal Rights in Scotland' by Sarah-Jane Macdonald
'A Practical Guide to New Build Conveyancing' by Paul Sams & Rebecca East
'A Practical Guide to Inherited Wealth on Divorce' by Hayley Trim
'A Practical Guide to Practice Direction 12J and Domestic Abuse in Private Law Children Proceedings' by Rebecca Cross & Malvika Jaganmohan
'A Practical Guide to Confiscation and Restraint' by Narita Bahra QC, John Carl Townsend, David Winch
'A Practical Guide to the Law of Forests in Scotland' by Philip Buchan
'A Practical Guide to Health and Medical Cases in Immigration Law' by Rebecca Chapman & Miranda Butler
'A Practical Guide to Bad Character Evidence for Criminal Practitioners by Aparna Rao
'A Practical Guide to Extradition Law post-Brexit' by Myles Grandison et al
'A Practical Guide to Hoarding and Mental Health for Housing Lawyers' by Rachel Coyle

'Stephens on Contractual Indemnities' by Richard Stephens

'A Practical Guide to the EU Succession Regulation' by Richard Frimston

'A Practical Guide to Solicitor and Client Costs – Second Edition' by Robin Dunne

'Constructive Dismissal – Practice Pointers and Principles' by Benjimin Burgher

'A Practical Guide to Religion and Belief Discrimination Claims in the Workplace' by Kashif Ali

'A Practical Guide to the Law of Medical Treatment Decisions' by Ben Troke

'Fundamental Dishonesty and QOCS in Personal Injury Proceedings: Law and Practice' by Jake Rowley

'A Practical Guide to the Law in Relation to School Exclusions' by Charlotte Hadfield & Alice de Coverley

'A Practical Guide to Divorce for the Silver Separators' by Karin Walker

'The Right to be Forgotten – The Law and Practical Issues' by Melissa Stock

'A Practical Guide to Planning Law and Rights of Way in National Parks, the Broads and AONBs' by James Maurici QC, James Neill et al

'A Practical Guide to Election Law' by Tom Tabori

'A Practical Guide to the Law in Relation to Surrogacy' by Andrew Powell

'A Practical Guide to Claims Arising from Fatal Accidents – Second Edition' by James Patience

'A Practical Guide to Asbestos Claims' by Jonathan Owen & Gareth McAloon

'A Practical Guide to Stamp Duty Land Tax in England and Northern Ireland' by Suzanne O'Hara

'A Practical Guide to the Law of Farming Partnerships' by Philip Whitcomb

'A Practical Guide to the Law of Unlawful Eviction and Harassment – Second Edition' by Stephanie Lovegrove

'A Practical Guide to Costs in Personal Injury Claims – Second Edition' by Matthew Hoe

'A Practical Guide to the General Data Protection Regulation (GDPR) – Second Edition' by Keith Markham

'A Practical Guide to Working with Litigants in Person and McKenzie Friends in Family Cases' by Stuart Barlow

'Protecting Unregistered Brands: A Practical Guide to the Law of Passing Off' by Lorna Brazell

'A Practical Guide to Secondary Liability and Joint Enterprise Post-Jogee' by Joanne Cecil & James Mehigan

'A Practical Guide to the Pre-Action RTA Claims Protocol for Personal Injury Lawyers' by Antonia Ford

'A Practical Guide to Neighbour Disputes and the Law' by Alexander Walsh

'A Practical Guide to Coercive Control for Legal Practitioners and Victims' by Rachel Horman

'A Practical Guide to the Law of Driverless Cars – Second Edition'

by Alex Glassbrook, Emma Northey & Scarlett Milligan

'A Practical Guide to TOLATA Claims' by Greg Williams

'A Practical Guide to Elderly Law – Second Edition' by Justin Patten

'A Practical Guide to Responding to Housing Disrepair and Unfitness Claims' by Iain Wightwick

'A Practical Guide to the Law of Bullying and Harassment in the Workplace' by Philip Hyland

'How to Be a Freelance Solicitor: A Practical Guide to the SRA-Regulated Freelance Solicitor Model' by Paul Bennett

'A Practical Guide to Prison Injury Claims' by Malcolm Johnson

'A Practical Guide to Advising Clients at the Police Station' by Colin Stephen McKeown-Beaumont

'A Practical Guide to Antisocial Behaviour Injunctions – Second Edition' by Iain Wightwick

'Practical Mediation: A Guide for Mediators, Advocates, Advisers, Lawyers, and Students in Civil, Commercial, Business, Property, Workplace, and Employment Cases' by Jonathan Dingle with John Sephton

'The Mini-Pupillage Workbook' by David Boyle

'A Practical Guide to Crofting Law' by Brian Inkster

'A Practical Guide to the Law of Domain Names and Cybersquatting' by Andrew Clemson

'A Practical Guide to the Law of Gender Pay Gap Reporting' by Harini Iyengar

'NHS Whistleblowing and the Law' by Joseph England

'Employment Law and the Gig Economy' by Nigel Mackay & Annie Powell

'A Practical Guide to Noise Induced Hearing Loss (NIHL) Claims' by Andrew Mckie, Ian Skeate, Gareth McAloon

'An Introduction to Beauty Negligence Claims – A Practical Guide for the Personal Injury Practitioner' by Greg Almond

'Intercompany Agreements for Transfer Pricing Compliance' by Paul Sutton

'Zen and the Art of Mediation' by Martin Plowman

'A Practical Guide to Adoption for Family Lawyers' by Graham Pegg

‘A Practical Guide to Industrial Disease Claims’ by Andrew Mckie & Ian Skeate

‘A Practical Guide to Conducting a Sheriff Court Proof’ by Andrew Stevenson

‘A Practical Guide to Vicarious Liability’ by Mariel Irvine

‘A Practical Guide to Applications for Landlord’s Consent and Variation of Leases’ by Mark Shelton

‘A Practical Guide to Relief from Sanctions Post-Mitchell and Denton’ by Peter Causton

‘A Practical Guide to Equity Release for Advisors’ by Paul Sams

‘A Practical Guide to Financial Services Claims’ by Chris Hegarty

‘A Practical Guide to Financial Ombudsman Service Claims’ by Adam Temple & Robert Scrivenor

‘A Practical Guide to Running Housing Disrepair and Cavity Wall Claims – Second Edition’ by Andrew Mckie & Ian Skeate

‘A Practical Guide to Holiday Sickness Claims – Second Edition’ by Andrew Mckie & Ian Skeate

‘Arguments and Tactics for Personal Injury and Clinical Negligence Claims’ by Dorian Williams

‘A Practical Guide to Drone Law’ by Rufus Ballaster, Andrew Firman, Eleanor Clot

‘On Experts: CPR35 for Lawyers and Experts’ by David Boyle

‘An Introduction to Personal Injury Law’ by David Boyle

These books and more are available to order online direct from the publisher at www.lawbriefpublishing.com, where you can also read free sample chapters. For any queries, call us on 0844 587 2383 or email us at mail@lawbriefpublishing.com.

Our books are all generally in stock at www.amazon.co.uk with free next day delivery for Prime members, and at good legal bookshops such as Wildy & Sons.

We are regularly launching new books in our series of practical day-to-day practitioners' guides. Visit our website and join our free newsletter to be kept informed and to receive special offers, free chapters, etc.

You can also follow us on Twitter at www.twitter.com/lawbriefpub.

www.ingramcontent.com/pod-product-compliance
Lightning Source LLC
LaVergne TN
LVHW022112200926
848481LV00003B/1143